CITY
WITHIN A
STATE

ANTHONY HILTON

CITY WITHIN A STATE

A Portrait of Britain's Financial World

I.B. TAURIS & Co Ltd
Publishers
London

Published by I.B.Tauris & Co. Ltd.
3 Henrietta Street
Covent Garden
London WC2E 8PW

British Library Cataloguing in Publication Data

Hilton, Anthony
   City within a state : a portrait of Britain's
   financial world.
   1. Financial institutions—England—
   London   2. Money market—England—London
   I. Title
   332.1'09421'2   HG186.G7

   ISBN 1-85043-044-6

Printed and bound in Great Britain by
Redwood Burn Limited, Trowbridge, Wiltshire.

CONTENTS

Preface

'Serious Money' was the title of a stage play popular in London in the summer of 1987. A satire on the City, London's financial centre, it was not the stuff of which stage dramas are usually made. Indeed in any previous age, it would probably have been a dramatic flop.

The fact that the play was put on at all was therefore significant. That it then played to packed houses was even more so, because it highlighted a growing public awareness of the City. It suggested that the rest of Britain was waking up to the notion that something was happening in the country's financial community – something they did not know about, which they did not understand, but which they nevertheless suspected was having a profound impact on the fabric of British life.

This book sets out to explain what is happening to the City – the heart of Britain's financial world. It shows that the City does handle 'serious money' – more than £100 billion changes hands every day in the foreign-exchange market alone – and explains why. It shows that more money is being made than ever before, and describes how this is done. And it sets out to show what is going on, and how a service industry can thrive so visibly – employment in the financial sector has expanded from under 7 per cent to over 10 per cent of the labour force in the first eight

Thatcher years – when there is less and less manufacturing industry to service.

This book looks at what the City is and does, not in an
economic or a purely financial sense, but from the perspective of those whom the City affects – be they the public, the
government and the politicians, or the City's customers at
home and abroad. It examines the trends which have given
the City an unprecedented burst of profitability, and asks
whether this is sustainable, or whether London will ultimately be swamped by the rival financial powers of New
York and Tokyo. It asks whether those outside the City
should be rooting for its success, or whether they should be
on the side of the United States and Japan.

The book demonstrates that the City operates on a global
front as well as on the domestic stage, providing services to
foreign governments and corporations much more than to
domestic clients. In an age of unprecedented economic turmoil the City takes a percentage cut of the huge capital
flows that stem from trade imbalances and from financial
volatility. It is thriving much as drug companies prosper in
an epidemic. The book shows how this has come about, and
how it results in huge profits for Britain from the selling of
banking, insurance and other financial services. But it also
reveals that this activity has a cost, and it is a cost which
falls on the rest of the country.

The book examines the real attitude of the City institutions to the government, to their clients in industry, and to
members of the public. It demonstrates how the pressures
on those who work in the City are often incompatible with
the desire of industrialists and politicians for cheap capital
and a quiet life. In some respects industry has suffered at
the hands of the City. In others industry has brought its
problems on itself.

The book scrutinises the level of integrity and honesty in
the City, and describes the techniques used in areas like
fund management and stock exchange trading, which have
frequently been used to ensure that the outside investor is
taken advantage of, and the City's profits boosted at the
client's expense. It expresses doubts about whether the
new regulatory structures erected under the 1986 Finan-

cial Services Act will substantially change the balance of power between those inside and outside the club.

The way the City influences political life in Britain is also examined. The book puts into perspective the limited role of financial contributions to the various political parties, and investigates instead the discreet behind-the-scenes lobbying through which the City has got its way in the past, and the autonomy with which it has often behaved. It shows how many people, including many politicians, regard the City as symbolising Mrs Thatcher's Britain. To her political opponents the City Yuppies with their six-figure salaries, Porsche cars, and liking for champagne bars represent the ugly side of the Thatcher revolution. And yet relations between the Government and the City are worse now than they have been for decades.

The book also demonstrates, in an examination of the role of the City abroad, and the perspective foreign countries bring to bear on it, how the City makes its own policy, often with scant regard for the professed desires of the government. It shows how City bankers, in their role of adviser and lender to foreign governments still exert considerable sway over the conduct of foreign affairs.

The breakdown of the world economic order in the 1970s has created a need in the international business community for some form of protection against the violent daily swings of the financial markets, currencies and interest rates – a protection which was formerly provided by agreement between governments and central bankers. That new protection has come from the City, which means in effect that the global financial system has been privatised. The book therefore sets out to discover who, in the absence of governments, now controls the levers of financial power, which ultimately govern all our destinies. It highlights how that power is derived, and the channels through which it is exercised. It shows the healthy side – how the City's traditional family and old boy networks have been overwhelmed by the influx of foreign firms and the need to recruit talent wherever it can be found. And it shows the risks – the UK government securities market, where British Governments raise their loans, is now dominated by

non-British firms with no allegiance or responsibility to
Westminster. It also demonstrates the resilience of the
City establishment and how even in the midst of unprecedented turmoil it is putting down new roots and seeking
to reassert its grip on City life.

Those who work in the Square Mile dismiss criticism of
the City as the politics of envy, but most serious commentators believe there is more to it than that. The times are
surely out of kilter when the starting salaries offered to the
cream of Oxbridge graduates by Britain's industrial companies are barely a third of what they can get from an
investment bank in the City; when the company which
produces all those Porsches itself makes more profit from
dealings in the currency and financial markets than it does
from selling the cars; when Hitachi of Japan, the most
powerful company in the most successful economy, still
makes one third of its profits from stock market dealing;
and when the financiers in the City are invariably so much
better-off than their customers, the people and businesses
they supposedly serve.

In conclusion, the aim of the book is to show how the City
fits into and interacts with the rest of British society,
exactly how it exerts its influence on politicians, industry
and the public at large, what it has to do to maintain its
position in the world, and whether at the end of the day its
activities are good or bad for Britain. Ultimately such
issues will be matters for the reader to judge. All I can do
as author is to provide some insights which will help inform this judgement, and to hope that, even when I fail to
provide the right answers, at least I ensure that in future
the right questions are asked.

Finally I should say that this book would never have
seen the light of day were it not for the support and hard
work of three people: my publisher Iradj Bagherzade who
originated the idea of this book; my editor Margaret Cor-
nell who gave the project form and logic, and Cyndy Miles
who provided far more support and encouragement in its
long period of gestation than I had any right to expect.

1

Can the City Survive?

There is in New York a large fund of British money deposited by the authorities of Lloyd's, the London insurance market, on the eve of the outbreak of the Second World War. It was moved across the Atlantic as the storm clouds threatened over Europe, to convince the Americans that whatever happened in the coming war between Britain and Germany, and even if Hitler's tanks were one day to roll into the courtyard of the Bank of England, the American clients of Lloyd's would not be affected. The fund in New York was the City's way of telling them that even defeat in a war would not be allowed to interfere with business. Americans with claims against policies at Lloyd's could be assured that, if their claims were just, they would be met in full as they had always been, only now the cash would come out of the pool in Manhattan. The money is still there, invested in the main in US government bonds, and has grown large over the years. The prospect of war may now seem remote to most people in Western Europe, and indeed to most people in Lloyd's. But the fund still proves good for business, giving reassurance to important US customers, and Lloyd's has never seen the need to bring the cash back.

This episode epitomises the City of London. It underlines how the City is international in its scope and thinks on a

global scale. It underlines how the City institutions put
their own interests first. And it reminds the rest of the
country, often brutally and tactlessly, that there is no
reason why it should consider doing anything else.

What is the City?

It is important to establish at the outset what we mean by
the City. Traditionally it was the area within the Roman
walls, and from that it came to be the financial community
within that square mile. In recent years, particularly in
the popular mind and in the world of politics, the City has
come to be synonymous with anything financial – be it a
business scandal or the activities of building societies. But
this is unhelpful and has caused irritation to many who
work in the City, who feel they are frequently blamed for
the sins of others.

The most helpful definition therefore is to use the City as
a term for those financial activities which are based, or
primarily based, in the financial community in London, of
which there are three immediately observable sub-divisions.
The first is the market-related activity of the community, be
it the Stock Exchange, Lloyd's of London, the London Futures and Options Exchange, the Baltic Exchange or the
London International Financial Futures Exchange.

Second is the banking industry, taking in the traditional
British commercial and clearing banks, the merchant
banks, and the hundreds of foreign banks which use London as a base for their international money-lending activities. And third are the City practices of the legal and
accountancy professions, which have flourished in recent
years as the City itself has flourished. Taken together,
these three interweave to form the financial structure
known throughout the world as the City.

Independence and self-interest

It is normal practice for the financial sector of any country
to put its own international interest before the interests of
the domestic economy. But not even the avowedly capital-

ist United States has allowed its financial community as much freedom and licence to pursue its own interest as successive British governments have given the City. From the City's perspective this has brought advantages. The independence of the City and its financiers from the whims and wishes of government helped first to create, and then to heighten, the image and the reality of pragmatism for which the British have become known around the world. And it made Britain unique in that it provided an alternative sphere for the exercise of domestic power, and meant that there were relatively few clashes between the wealth-generating elite and the political bureaucracy. Viewed from abroad, this underlined the attractions of the City as a place where business could be done without fear of political interference.

Money knows no politics, and the City's clear understanding of this has led to its being respected and trusted by other nations, even when their governments are at loggerheads with Whitehall. Few foreign investors believe, for example, that the City would allow the government to freeze the bank deposits of a foreign country as the Americans under President Carter froze the deposits of Iran during the hostage crisis.

The reality is not quite as clear-cut. Though in the First World War it took two years before financial links betwen British banks and Germany were fully severed, there was no such hiatus in the Second. Nevertheless, the City does tend to take smaller skirmishes in its stride. In the Falklands hostilities with Argentina in 1982, while high-profile financial transactions like international lending were slowed down or put on ice at an official level, much of the low-profile business continued as usual; Lloyds Bank, which has a vast network of banks in that country, continued to trade there normally. The structure of the lending between the two countries was such that Britain stood to lose much more than Argentina if it declared financial war, and this probably helped the government to accept that there was little point in a freeze. Nevertheless, as the high-profile business also resumed within weeks of the cessation of hostilities – in undue haste, in Mrs Thatcher's view – it helped underline what foreign governments believe is the City's independence. It was also this belief which, two years previously, led to the Bank of England playing a key role in the release of the American hostages; it was trusted by the Iranians, the Algerians and the Americans to handle the vast sums of money which needed to be transferred to bring an end to the crisis.

In the beginning the separation of political from financial power mattered little as Britain was pre-eminent in both. But as Britain's industrial and political influence declined, the separateness of the City took on a different dimension. The City continued as it always had done to pursue its own narrow interest, but the difference in the latter part of the twentieth century was that the rest of the country could no longer hold its own, and could cope less and less with the shocks to the economic and political fabric caused by the self-serving actions of the City. This was particularly evident during the takeover boom of the 1980s which led to accusations from industrialists of the stature of the Chairman of ICI, Sir John Harvey-Jones, and the Chancellor of the Exchequer, Nigel Lawson, that the City was thinking too short-term, and damaging the health of the industrial sector as a result. Relations between the City and industry reached such a low ebb in 1986 that the Confederation of British Industry set up a working party to try to build bridges between the two sides – but with little prospect of real long-term success, given the diversity of power and interest between the two sectors.

The City regards itself as separate from the country at large, and sees the actions of governments as somehow not binding on it. Though the motto of the Stock Exchange, 'Dictum meum Pactum – My word is my bond', is designed to underline the integrity of the City and the belief that the spirit of the law is much more important than the letter, the City does not always apply this maxim when responding to the laws of the land. At a time when industry was prohibited from putting money overseas by rigid post-war exchange controls, the leading firms in the City could usually get clearance from the Bank of England to channel funds wherever and whenever they wanted, regardless of the fact that the national interest as defined by government decreed that the money should have stayed within Britain's shores. On a much smaller scale, when successive Chancellors of the Exchequer developed business expansion schemes and equity investment plans, designed to encourage serious industrial investment in return for tax reliefs, the City turned these into tax shelters for its own practitioners and favoured clients, and thereby undermined their intention.

Most of all, the City's indifference to the wider impact of its actions, and the fact that these might contravene the spirit if not the letter, not only of the law of the land, but of the principle of free markets by which it professes to live, showed through in the massive share-ramping exercises which became a feature of takeover bids in the 1980s. These culminated in the Guinness affair of 1986, when a team of City advisers, together with key directors of Guinness, organised a massive share-buying programme, artificially to inflate the price of Guinness shares in a contested bid for Distillers. The manipulation took place undetected right under the noses of the authorities and involved some of the top City names. When details began to emerge the City authorities did nothing, and it was only the appointment of Department of Trade and Industry inspectors – the exercise of power from outside the City – which forced the affair into the open. In the months of press speculation and leaks which followed, the City's silence continued. There was barely a single press statement from the Takeover Panel or the Stock Exchange, the two bodies most intimately involved. In the United States the regulators would have seized the opportunity to clean out the stable. In the City the automatic instinct of the Stock Exchange was to keep a low profile and do nothing but wait for the affair to blow over, in the hope that it could then resume business as normal.

Successful abroad

International its actions are, self-serving its motives may be, but perhaps precisely because of these characteristics

the City provides services the world needs and is prepared
to pay for. Today, in spite of unprecedented levels of competition from the United States and Japan, it remains the
lead player on the world financial stage in a whole range of
activities. Given the volatility of world finance, this is a
truly remarkable achievement.

Britain is a small country compared to the United
States, the Soviet Union, China, Japan, or even France or
Germany. It has little economic and diminishing political
influence on the world stage. It is only loosely attached to
Europe, in spite of many years of membership of the European Economic Community. Nevertheless, the City still
dominates international banking and British banks still
account for a larger share of loans to third countries and
third markets than any other nation. It is the home of
Eurobond trading – the issuing of foreign currency bonds –
and has fostered that market to the extent that it is now
the world's biggest debt market, outstripping even that of
the United States. It is easily the world centre in foreign-
exchange dealing, with a daily turnover half as much
again as New York and with an even greater margin over
Tokyo, Hong Kong and Zurich. It is still the world centre
for insurance, both through Lloyd's of London, the leading
specialist insurance market, and through the dominance of
companies like Commercial Union and Royal Insurance
which remain among the largest in the world. Its gold
market vies with that of Zurich and its commodity markets
share the world leadership with those in New York. It
provides the only alternative financial futures market of
consequence to those of Chicago, though, to be realistic, it
lags so far behind in this area that it is not yet a force in
world terms.

Most significant of all, it has carried out a series of
fundamental reforms – the so-called Big Bang – to position
it so that it can become the world centre for trading in
international securities. This is a still developing skill and
involves the selling to investors all over the world of the
shares of the leading companies – Sony from Japan, Fiat
from Italy, Philips from Holland, General Motors from the
United States. If it succeeds, it will assure London's

prosperity for decades. But, precisely because international securities trading promises to become the major part of world financial business, if the City fails to get its share, its strength in other areas will not save it from a decline which will ultimately turn London into little more than a financial colony of the United States or Japan.

Thus far, however, the City has clearly provided the world with a range of services that it wants and which it has not been able to obtain elsewhere. This could not have been achieved in the first place without the application of a considerable amount of talent. And it certainly could not have been preserved without considerable tenacity and a willingness to fight for business in international markets, which belies the City stereotype of gentlemanly and sometimes effete behaviour.

Unpopular at home

Its achievements are little appreciated, however, in the country which gives it its home, and the failure to build bridges with the rest of the country and with even friendly governments in Whitehall must count as one of the central weaknesses in the City's position. The rest of the country, and indeed many of the Westminster politicians, regard the financial centre as an offshore island on the Thames, more like an unsunny version of the Cayman Islands rather than a great national asset to be treasured and nurtured. Even Conservative party members from the top leadership down, whom one would expect to be the natural allies of bankers and financiers, declare themselves embarrassed or outraged by the City, by the salaries it pays and by its relentless pursuit of money-making.

It could be argued that this is short-sighted of the politicians, but the City is not to be outdone and holds politicians of all parties in almost equal contempt for their duplicity and lack of principle. By the actions of its institutions it has almost perversely gone out of its way to encourage the divide and seems almost happy to accept a role in which domestic affairs play little part. Even the City's traditional regulator, the Bank of England – a nationalised body and therefore, one would have thought, part of the government machine – is so distanced from Whitehall that it frames its memoranda to other government departments, whatever the legislation, in the context of what is good for the City's international reputation, not its domestic role. It took the creation of a totally new body, the Securities and Investments Board, which was set up in 1986 to enforce the laws enshrined in the new Financial Services Act, to bring to the City a perspective of what was expected of it by those outside. To some extent this perspective modified the views of the Bank of England, but its prime concern remained to ensure that nothing was done which might harm the international image of the City. The fact that its domestic image was tarnished was not, until the Guinness affair, an issue that merited serious consideration.

This detachment of the City is particularly regrettable because it is socially divisive. The leading lights of the City are paid on an international scale, which bears comparison with salaries for their kind of expertise anywhere in the world. But this means that they earn sums which are totally beyond the comprehension of the typical British industrial manager or entrepreneur. It therefore reinforces a cultural divide in Britain between those who make money and those who make things. This acts as a magnet drawing off the best talent and leaving industry woefully short. The division is made worse by the accident of geography which has concentrated the City in the affluent South East and industry in the now less affluent Midlands and North.

The cumulative effect of these factors is to provide the conditions for a possible political backlash. Nor is this likely only with a left-wing government in Westminster. The passing of the Financial Services Act in 1986 imposes a hitherto unheard-of degree of regulation on the City. No one in the City denies that the law on investor protection needed updating. But the costs and restrictions of the structures created by the Financial Services Act and the City's lack of success in lobbying against them have caused it considerable concern. It worries in particular that the new Securities and Investments Board may well be a Trojan horse for comprehensive detailed regulation of City activities the moment the government can find a pretext for such action.

Given that the City is successful and prosperous largely because of the free-wheeling approach it has been able to adopt, it can be argued that tighter regulation is in neither its best interests nor those of the country. But the City has worked inadequately at its own public relations to head off a backlash, and it is this lack of foresight in defining and protecting its own interests which it may well come to regret as the twentieth century draws to a close.

The opening up of the club

Reflecting on the recent opening up of the City, one leading merchant banker remarked, 'All change in the City is a mistake, especially change for the better'.[1] He was mourning the passing of the traditional way of doing business. The unique *modus operandi* of the City, with its heavy reliance on independence from statutory control linked to the principle of internal self-regulation, its emphasis on informality and personal contact at the highest levels of decision-taking, and the extraordinarily close-knit nature of the financial community, has been essential to its success in the past. But it is precisely these characteristics that cause the City's detractors to regard it as an anachronism or at best an exclusive club where membership bestows on a privileged few a divine right to make money. It is an impression that the City, with its periodic outbreaks of greed as displayed by the Guinness affair, does little to dispel.

It has certainly been the case for generations that there was little freedom of entry to the inner circles of the City, except for the exceptionally talented whom it could not ignore. The bankers, the brokers, the discount houses and the Stock Exchange formed themselves into associations, and in return for drawing up rules of good conduct secured the blessing of the Bank of England, whose task it was to keep a watching eye and help keep the City clean. From there it was just a short step to using association membership as a device to keep out newcomers – particularly newcomers who threatened to be too competitive – and to preserve the cartels, and the profits which flowed from them, for the benefit of those who were already within the club. It meant that those lucky enough to work in the City were guaranteed to be prosperous, as long as the monopoly could be preserved; and because they were prosperous, its defenders argue, they tended also to be honest, to police themselves effectively and to weed out or exclude those whose actions threatened to undermine the system. Critics say that the honesty was circumscribed; that while clients were rarely systematically disadvantaged, there were few restraints on people working in the City to prevent their using the information they gleaned for their own benefit. Inevitably too, because of the exclusiveness of the club, they became self-selecting groups dominated by people from the same few families, the same narrow class and similar social and educational background.

The power of the City is therefore one of the least understood features of modern Britain. It gained this astonishing power largely by accident of history, but it has preserved it by the ruthless exploitation of monopoly, and a determination not to allow foreign competition to gain a foothold in its markets. Now, however, the world has caught up with the City and the pressures of change on the international stage have brought the barriers tumbling down.

What has surprised even the Americans, who have been the major force trying to gain entry to the City's financial markets, is that City institutions which had been protected for so long did respond at the eleventh hour. When they finally saw that the old ways could not survive, and that the strategy of changing the world to suit the City was no longer tenable, they changed themselves.

In an astonishingly short time in the early 1980s every tradition which got in the way of survival was ruthlessly jettisoned, and new international houses were created out of an amalgam of the traditionally separate City firms, in many cases with the capital to finance the mergers coming from outside collaborators. None of these were Japanese, as the Bank of England quietly discouraged City firms from forming alliances with them,[2] and they were forced to establish themselves independently from scratch. But many of the big American, European, Far Eastern and Australian banks came into the securities markets at this point, as did the major British banks like Barclays, National Westminster and Midland. They faced tremendous problems of management in integrating the new financial conglomerates, but these were addressed with a vigour and a single-minded determination which were in total contrast to what had gone before. No other aspect of British life embraced the need for violent and often unpleasant change so readily. It is ironic that the City, which is seen popularly as a major bastion of conservatism, underwent a transformation of attitudes far more radical and far-reaching than any other section of British society.

Whether it will be enough, remains to be seen. There are precedents of countries living by their financial wits rather than their industrial skills. There is nevertheless a danger that the American and Japanese firms now operating in the City could prove too powerful for the native British firms. They have a much larger home base into which the British firms have barely penetrated, and the strength of their economies might eventually give them the muscle in their British operations to overwhelm the British-owned City firms and bring an end to their independence. But even if the institutions fall into non-British hands, the City will remain as a financial centre and the footsoldiers will be British as they are now. They may be mercenaries, however, for foreign organisations, and the ultimate benefit of their skills, the profits they earn, will flow to other countries.

While it may be possible for a financial centre to exist without the backing of a powerful economy, it has not been achieved successfully before, because profits earned at home are what makes success possible and affordable in foreign markets. The British economy does not look powerful enough to generate the profits the securities houses need. Figures produced by Christopher Johnson, economic adviser to Lloyds Bank,[3] underline how difficult it is for the City to fight in this league now that the US economy is nine times as large as the British economy and the Japanese three times the size.

Bank lending in Britain, ignoring inter-bank lending, was just over £180 billion ('000 million) in 1985. Of this nearly a quarter went to individuals as personal lending (the most buoyant sector), a tenth into government debt and the other two-thirds to business. Domestic bank lending in America was eight times as large and in Japan it was six times, so the profits engine available to those banks from domestic operations was significantly greater.

The value of equities quoted on the Stock Exchange at the end of 1985 was roughly £250 billion, more than twice the total of bank loans to business borrowers, and in 1985 new bank loans, at £15 billion, were three times the value of new equity issues. Japanese equities were worth two and a half times as much as the British and US equities seven times as much. In 1986–7 this gap has widened further, as the Tokyo market in particular soared to quite unprecedented highs.

There is very little activity in the UK corporate bond market, where there is just £8 billion of issues outstanding. But the US corporate bond market was worth $740 billion in 1985, and in that year alone it handled net new issues worth $100 billion. In Tokyo the corporate bond market is roughly half the size of the American.

Even the government securities market, where the City has a justifiable reputation, proves to be a minnow by world standards. The figures are these. In the UK outstanding gilts totalled £127 billion at the end of 1985 ($183 billion). The US Treasury market was some five and a half times the size and had topped $1 trillion (million million). The Japanese market was three and a half times the British. At the same time the US and Japanese securities houses have huge agency, state and municipal bond markets to trade in, which have more debt in issue than the central government. The UK local authority loan market in contrast is very small.

Where London does score is in international banking. The Eurobanking market in the City was nearly $600 billion at the end of 1985, or twice the size of the domestic banking market mentioned earlier. This gave it a market share of one-fifth of the total world market, against one-seventh for American banks and about half that for Tokyo. But though it operates out of London, this market is no longer dominated by British banks. In fact, the Japanese account for 30 per cent of the assets in the Eurobanking market, the British 17 per cent and the Americans 16 per cent.

In addition to international banking, there is of course the international bond market. This is now more active than banking, with a 1985 net new issue total of $125 billion. The size of this Eurobond market at $355 billion is similar to the London equity market, but is growing much faster.

London is also the world leader in foreign exchange where the daily turnover in 1985 was $90 billion compared with $48 billion in New York and $45 billion in Tokyo. Many of these transactions are between banks and only about one-tenth of them are believed to be generated by underlying trade flows.

So what this means is that London can live by its wits to an extent, but the areas where it does so are those of ferocious competition and high risk. What it really needs to survive in the medium term is a much expanded domestic base, substantially larger than Britain alone can provide. And that of course is why some firms have begun to expand into continental Europe, and why many policy-makers in the Bank of England favour greater European financial union. They believe that if London can be established as the financial centre for the Europe-wide industrial machine, then it might indeed have a chance of holding its own against the other two global financial centres.

The central issue facing the City today is simply one of survival. It prospered in the past when it operated as a collection of what were in effect cottage industries, and chose its people from a narrow social band. It developed skills which exploited its contacts to the full, and gave it an image of integrity in the world at large. But this was not achieved without costs, which include the political isolation of the City and the distrust and active dislike of many people in the industrial and commercial sectors of the British economy.

The foundation of the City's traditional strength, power and influence have now suddenly crumbled. The financial market has become international and the walls which were sufficient to keep out domestic competition have proved inadequate to withstand the blasts from abroad. The elitist structures have been broken down and the new institutions hastily erected to take their place have neither the strength nor the authority to preserve the old privileges.

Can the City live by its wits without protection and without the power that comes from a massive industrial hinterland? Can it justify its wealth and power by proving to be the best in the world in what it does? And does it really matter to the country at large what happens to the City? Does the City deserve special treatment and should its interests come first even when what is good for the City can have adverse repercussions elsewhere in the economy? Has the City been good for the country in the past, and is its economic, social and political influence such that the country will ensure its prosperity in the future? These are the questions which will be addressed in the following chapters of this book.

2

The Old Fighting the New

The changes in the City in the 1980s set the stage for a classic battle between the old world and the new. At first glance the established order had been defeated, overwhelmed by the weight of foreign money which gobbled up its serried ranks of small businesses. But a closer examination suggests that such a judgement may be premature. Uprooted it certainly had been, but within months of Big Bang the establishment plant was putting down roots into the new soil, and promising to reform itself, spread more thinly perhaps but none the less tenaciously throughout the new world.

In this it was helped by the fact that it is one of the most entrenched sections of British society. The City establishment is not just a question of blood, it is a state of mind, a whole way of doing business, a complete approach to the world. Such ingrained beliefs do not change simply because the context changes. Indeed, as we shall see in the pages which follow, the very ethos of several of the top-flight City firms is so rooted in its network of contacts that they could not change even if they wanted to. For this unchanging inner core the going will certainly be tough; the lesson of others, less rigid, or probably less durable, is that the style has to change. But even this poses a question. Do the organisations have a culture separate from the people who work in them, as most

City people believe? If they do, who will come out on top?
Will the people mould the organisations or will the organisations change the people? In the past the City's organisations
have always changed and absorbed the outsiders. Can they
do it again, in the face of their biggest challenge?

Whom you know

Although it wielded tremendous economic and social power, the typical City firm, whether merchant bank, broker
or discount house, was, until the late 1980s, a small family
business. A handful of huge insurance companies and
clearing banks were exceptions, since they were deeply
involved in insuring and financing international trade and
therefore saw the world as their market. Though even here
– witness the Mountain family at Eagle Star and the Bevan and Tuke families at Barclays Bank – it was quite
possible well into the 1980s for the firms to be global and
still be run by the founding family. Such size was unusual,
however, and when it came to servicing the domestic economy the City was a collection of cottage industries, each
offering a highly specialised service.

Such a system put the emphasis on individual relationships rather than individual abilities, because almost
all business was obtained by referral and by exploiting
long-term friendships and associations built up over many
years. It was also established practice to return 'favours',
with those who were owed the biggest favour obtaining the
pick of the best deals. It was therefore very difficult for any
outsider to break in, unless he happened to be a person of
quite exceptional talent and determination; a successful
career in the City was very much in the gift of the established City families.

The story of Sir Peter Tapsell, a partner in James Capel,
one of the big City stockbrokers, and a Tory MP, illustrates
this.[1] He got his start immediately after the war in a
discount house, because his mother was a friend of the
mistress of the top man there – a legendary City figure
called A. W. Trinder. When he tried to move on he came up
against Lionel Fraser at Schroders, who turned him down

because he had not been to Eton; neither had Fraser, but he told Tapsell it had taken him twenty years to acquire the self-confidence and contacts which every old Etonian has as of right. Lord Cromer, the head of Barings, the oldest City merchant bank, was equally blunt – telling him the only way he would get to the top was 'to marry one of these', indicating with a sweep of his hand pictures of unmarried Barings daughters. Tapsell then abandoned his merchant banking ambitions and turned instead to the less elitist world of stockbroking, where Trinder's recommendation was sufficient to secure him a place as a clerk in the then quite small office of James Capel. He ultimately became a successful stockbroker, but in the wider confines of the City he always felt an outsider.

> The new boy can never have the self-confidence of an old boy, and the old boys know it. If you are a Hambro or a Rothschild you have done it for generations. Coming from the outside you can never have their arrogance.

Though stockbroking was considered less of a profession for gentlemen than merchant banking, it still helped greatly, when trying to get in from outside the City, to have a family connection. This was particularly true of the biggest firms like Cazenove and Rowe and Pitman. Cazenove, perhaps the most influential stockbroking firm in the post-war period, retains even in the 1980s the right of every partner to 'present' one son at the door of the firm for admission. A partnership at Cazenove is a gift to be coveted, for its people are among the highest paid in the City, with salaries in excess of £500,000 a year at 1985 prices commonplace among the partners.

But times have changed to the extent that entry to the firm is no longer an automatic route to success. The presentation does not have to be the eldest son – it is up to the father to choose which he thinks is the most suited to the work. If the father chooses wrongly he does not get a second chance, and nor does the son. One long-time Cazenove partner told me that he had personally fired four sons of partners who failed to make the grade, and he stressed that the pressure on sons was greater than on the rest of the

intake – 'they have to run 110 yards for every 100'.[2] There
is no guaranteed route to the top for the favoured sons; no
son of a senior partner has ever risen to be senior partner
himself in his turn since the nineteenth century.

It may be added that even in the 1980s the system has
never applied to daughters. And though Cazenove employs
as many women as any other broking firm, it still tries to
enforce its elitist principles. A woman graduate told me
how her interview – fixed up through a contact – consisted
of two questions: Where did she go to school and what did
her father do? She replied Cheltenham Ladies College, and
the director of a large public company. She got the job.[3]

Once in the firm everyone is treated equally, so that the
firm is a genuine meritocracy, according to Cazenove partners. The favouritism lies in getting in in the first place.
Though most partners are related in some way to the big
City families, there are partners who have risen from the
broking equivalent of the shop floor. Peter Smith, who
became one of the most respected men in the firm, joined
initially as a 15-year-old from the East End in the clerical
department before his talents were recognised and he was
given the chance to move up in the firm.

Cazenove partners also believe[4] that between them they
have relatives in most of the leading City firms, and particularly in the merchant banks, and this has led the firm to
behave with an arrogance which may have been fine when
the City was a village, but which is out of keeping with
modern times. Fund managers, the present-day financial
barons, complain bitterly that when Cazenove is trying to
sell shares in a company which appears overpriced, it simply tells them how many they will be allowed to buy. If they
protest they know they will not be given the opportunity to
buy shares in the next certain success. Market-makers
complain[5] that Cazenove partners will demand a favourable price for what they buy – a price not available to
others in the market – and will again use the threat of
future discrimination against the firm to obtain their privileges. They point out that though Cazenove has been
involved in promoting several investments which have
turned out disastrously – such as Acorn Computer, or *The*

Daily Telegraph – it has avoided censure by the Stock Exchange, prompting the widespread belief that the Council of the Exchange does not feel it has the authority to challenge the firm.[6] Cazenove even treated with disdain the censure it received from the City's Takeover Panel, a self-regulatory watchdog, in its conduct during the takeover battle for the engineering company AE, when share purchases which thwarted the bid were undisclosed, in apparent if unwitting contravention of the Takeover Code.

The system clearly has worked for Cazenove. Others found they did not have the contacts to maintain such a rigidly elitist stance. To some extent this makes Cazenove the anachronism, a firm whose days may be numbered, but the power of the firm and its patronage should not be underestimated. Alone among the big brokers it stayed independent post Big Bang by persuading a syndicate of investing institutions to make available to it, on favourable terms, all the capital it would need to operate in the new markets. The syndicate, known colloquially as the 'friends of Caz', guarantees the firm's ability not simply to stay independent, but to carry on doing business as it has always done – even when this means it behaves very much as a law unto itself, disdainful of the rules and codes applicable to lesser firms.

Other brokers worked assiduously to cultivate similar links before Big Bang brought about their absorption into larger impersonal conglomerates. Though it dates from the pre-war period, their philosophy in these ambitions has been summed up for good and all by Lancelot Hugh Smith, perhaps the greatest senior partner this century of Rowe and Pitman. His father had been Governor of the Bank of England and his family had founded the National Provincial Bank (the National in National Westminster), so he understood what he was writing about when he told his partners in the 1930s:[7]

> I have always felt that if they keep their heads up and their overheads down, a firm containing three members of great city families – Smith, Fleming, and Baring – must succeed.

What has changed in the 1980s is that it is now open to

firms without the family connections to forge links in other
ways, because the number of people working in the City
has expanded so fast that they no longer share a common
background. Instead, the links are forged on a lavish scale
at social events like Royal Ascot, Wimbledon and the Henley regatta, with institutional fund managers and other
favoured clients. Nor is the hospitality always respectable.
One broker, the son of a peer, organised a private screening
of one of the original pornographic movies, 'Deep Throat',
together with a guest appearance of its star Linda Love-
lace, for some fifty fund managers in an attempt to drum
up business.

The role of lunch

The old and the new world are at one, however, when it
comes to the importance of lunch. Traders and salesmen
may be lucky to grab a sandwich and glass of mineral
water at their dealing desks, but at 12.45 the heads of their
departments slip upstairs to what is still a different world.
Lunch remains the hub of City business and social life. The
typical merchant bank will have more than a dozen dining
rooms complete with in-house catering, where it entertains
clients, potential clients, businessmen, financial journalists, politicians, heads of foreign governments – indeed,
anyone with influence and contacts who could possibly be
of use to the firm. An invitation to lunch in some firms is
recognition that you have 'arrived', and are no longer an
outsider. The phrase 'we had him in to lunch' is used as a
reference, an endorsement, albeit limited, of the integrity
of the person concerned. Lunch is used to forge relationships, to cement deals, and (particularly with journalists) to resolve past differences and misunderstandings and
form the basis for a new forward-looking relationship.

Indeed, the City has a mystical belief in the healing
power of lunch, and this indirectly leads to its poor relationships with politicians in Westminster. It cannot understand how a politician whom it found civilised company
over the port, can turn round and attack it a few weeks or
months later. It would never expect such treatment from a

guest from the City, for that would undermine the basis of
trust which the lunch was intended to foster, the trust
being a necessary precursor of a business relationship.

The guest lists remain a secret, though not closely
guarded, on the ground that they give clues to future
business developments. The idea is that rivals must not be
helped to chase and develop the same contacts. That is also
the reason why the City has never supported gentlemen's
clubs, in the way in which they are meeting-places for the
professions and aristocracy in London's West End. Though
the appropriately named 'City Club' continues to make a
living, few City people would risk being seen there, let
alone possibly overheard, when lunching with a major
client.

Cultural divide

This mixing of the old and the new has also highlighted the
continuing cultural divide in the City, however, and the
difficulty inherent in getting teams from independent
backgrounds to work closely together. Lunch has also become a battleground, with different members of what is
now supposedly one firm refusing to sit at the same table,
not because of personal dislike, but through a lack of
appreciation of the other person's skills or their relevance.[8]
The Big Bang brought people of different backgrounds –
brokers, bankers and jobbers (or market-makers) –
together under one roof for the first time. Simultaneously
it added to their feelings of dislocation by abolishing the
separate functions in which the broker acted for clients and
principal, while the market-maker took risks and acted as
a wholesaler of shares. Now most firms combine both functions.

One of the difficulties in making these new units profitable is that there has always been a cultural divide between different sections of the City. Stockbrokers have
always looked down on stock jobbers, whom they thought
of as little better than tradesmen, making a living by
buying and selling. And in Britain's class-dominated society to be in trade was considered inferior to being a member

of a profession, which a stockbroker, as an adviser to clients, considered himself to be – even when, as was frequently the case, the heads of the jobbing firms were just as Etonian and blue-blooded as the brokers.

The brokers were in turn looked down upon by the merchant bankers. Anthony Hornby, a scion of the family which created W.H. Smith and whose nephew is its chairman, rebuilt Cazenove after the war by acknowledging this fact. Nationalisation of the electricity, railways and mining industries had robbed Cazenove of almost its entire client list, but Hornby restored the firm's fortunes by providing a service to the merchant banks which were then beginning to bring new companies to the market. He had one golden rule. If another broker wanted a meeting, no matter who he was, he came to Cazenove; but if a merchant banker, no matter how humble, wanted a consultation, Cazenove went to see him. This may sound trivial but it exemplified in the City's subtle way that Cazenove knew its place in the pecking order – the best of brokers, but not in the same league as the merchant banks. False modesty was out, but so too was false arrogance.

Hornby followed this rule himself, though he found walking difficult as a result of wartime injuries. And it is interesting also to note, now that one rarely, if ever, sees a bowler hat in the City, that right through to the 1970s he insisted that no member of Cazenove staff ever visited one of those merchant banks without wearing one. It was a rule he insisted on even when the partner concerned was simply visiting the chairman – his uncle – on a family matter.

The firms are bigger now. The numbers of people employed have soared. The activities are no longer separate, but in the most successful firms are being welded into a multi-functional service for clients. The markets are global, and the cottage industries have had to consolidate and grow to keep pace with them. But the same City names still occur again and again among the banks and brokers, and the top players often go back many generations. Lord Williams, unusual because he is a Labour peer in a very Conservative world, worked first for Barings and later became chairman of Henry Ansbacher, another merchant

bank; his mother was a Cazenove. Sir John Prideaux re-
tired recently after many years as chairman of National
Westminster Bank, and joined the board of Arbuthnot
Latham, another merchant bank; his mother was an
Arbuthnot. When Barclays Bank decided to move into the
stockbroking business, it paid £80 million for De Zoete and
Bevan; Barclay's chairman at the time was Sir Timothy
Bevan, a distant relative.

Elitism

Until the 1960s and the massive expansion of the City
caused by the influx of American, European and some
Japanese banks and securities houses, few outsiders managed to break in. The City therefore became dominated by
the people who had been to a very few of the top public
schools, most notably Eton, and in a few of the exclusive
regiments, usually the Guards. This made it elitist and
isolated from the influences and the thinking which
affected the rest of the country.

Because of their inter-marrying and common backgrounds and because the City occupies a very small geog-
raphical area – the Square Mile – everyone at the top
levels in the financial world knew everyone else. They may
even have known them at school twenty years before.
Typical was the Hon. Mervyn Greenway, a partner with
stockbroker Capel Cure Myers, who had two fags at Winchester: George Magan who became a leading figure in the
corporate finance department of Morgan Grenfell and
Nicholas Jones, active in corporate finance at Schroders
and later Lazards.[9] A director of Robert Fleming told me
without a hint of irony that X had been a bit of a rogue at
school and it would not surprise him at all if he was in
trouble with the Stock Exchange authorities now.[10] In the
same vein, when the Stock Exchange decided in the 1980s
to invite lay members on to its Council, one of the first to be
chosen was the former headmaster of Winchester.

This excessive familiarity, though it could be suffocat-
ing, had a strong practical benefit. People always knew
who they were dealing with and they could therefore

thrash out deals verbally without the contracts and legal documentation which tied up every transaction in the United States. The result was a system which, though incestuous, gave the City a flexibility which has allowed more quick-witted members full rein to make considerable fortunes. And those who broke their word did so at their peril. The news spread so quickly that there was no one left with whom they could do business.

Firms found increasingly after Big Bang and the huge increase in both the volume of trading and competitive pressures, that this system was breaking down. The legalisation of City dealings grew rapidly, the involvement of lawyers was reflected in a doubling over ten years in the number of partners in the big City law firms. Understandably, however, where the traces still existed, uncertainty helped renew and strengthen the importance of old ties. The life lines which remained to hand in the turbulent changes were seized as avidly as they had ever been. And there are many who predict that when the next round of rationalisation comes to the City, the first firms to seek to ensure their survival by banding together into still larger units will be those where there are still family links.

It is important to note, however, that this clannishness did not necessarily make the system honest in its dealings with the outside world. What it did was ensure that the City's people were honest with each other. But as the Guinness affair, and similar takeover scandals, have shown in the 1980s, it was not unusual for interest groups in the City to consort together in a way which, while it may not have been strictly illegal, was certainly calculated to deceive those on the outside.

The Guinness affair consisted of one bank, Morgan Grenfell, using its influence to persuade others, including Henry Ansbacher, to assist it in supporting the Guinness share price, in Guinness's bid for Distillers. Such mutual help was typical. When, for instance, a pension fund manager, outsider Geoffrey Musson, tried to take over Berry Trust, one of the leading investment trusts, a group of like-minded investment trust managers banded together and used the funds under their control to buy shares at above

the market price – taking a loss in order to thwart the bid.
Musson was philosophical about his defeat at the hands of
what he termed 'the old City club', on the basis that if the
club decided you would lose a bid there was little you, as a
non-club member, could do about it.[11] He recognised that it
was a common feature of the takeover scene, even in the
1980s, for defenders to organise fan clubs – fund managers
who will take a loss, as described above, in return for
favours in the future. Thus those with power and influence
are cultivated and can strengthen their position; those
without it are squeezed. It was the way the City had always worked in the past; and though diminished in the
extent of its influence by the changes of Big Bang, it was
the way the establishment could still, when the occasion
demanded, work in the 1980s.

On the surface it all seems very civilised, but appear-
ances are deceptive. The grapevine is still used, as it has
been in the past, to put people out of business whom the
established members do not like or see as a threat. For
instance, when Harvard Securities, the most successful of
the licensed dealers operating under remit as a dealer in
securities under the auspices of the Department of Trade
and Industry and therefore outside the control of the Stock
Exchange, applied to that body for membership, the Exchange's response was to send its founder, Tom Wilmot,
400 pages of press cuttings on his firm going back twelve
years, asking for detailed comments on each.[12] It did not
like Harvard's way of doing business, considering its sales
techniques aggressive and the stocks it promoted of low
quality. But rather than seek to control it and demand
improvements from the inside, the Exchange appeared to
prefer to pretend that the firm did not and should not exist.

Wilmot was not the first to suffer the establishment's
wrath. At the other extreme, Sir Siegmund Warburg,
founder of the City's most successful post-war merchant
bank, S.G. Warburg, has described how the City's existing
banks fought jealously to preserve their patch against outsiders. This they did by declining to take part in deals
dreamt up by the newcomer, advising clients not to take
part in such deals, and encouraging friends and relations

in ancillary firms to deny the services to the newcomer that he needed to make anything happen at all. They would use their financial muscle to sabotage his deals, pushing up the price of shares he needed to buy, or arranging for a friend or industrial contact to intervene to block a takeover, even if to do so acted against their short-term financial interests. Though competitive pressures played a great part in all this, it was also a crude sort of initiation ceremony – seeing how a newcomer coped with rough treatment served to prove whether or not he was worthy to be a member of the club.[13]

That the inner circle of merchant bankers – the core of the establishment – should use its influence to try to force out the bright immigrant was certainly ironic, given that the majority were themselves founded by immigrants. Though Warburg himself was convinced that much of the opposition was personal, others are less sure. They say it was simply business and a natural reaction to outside competition. Warburg rarely complained about the treatment he was given, but at times the bitterness showed. Towards the end of his life, in a rare interview in 1980 he spoke of how the City had regarded him:[14]

> as a damn foreigner . . . a German Jew . . . a fellow who speaks with a foreign accent, all that sort of thing. I remember some people in very good houses talked very nastily behind my back: 'Do you know this fellow Siegmund Warburg? He starts in the office at 8 o'clock in the morning'. That was considered contemptible. Most of them came to the office at 10 o'clock in the morning. I was awful. They looked down on me with the utmost snobbism.

The beginning of change

The lesson of Warburg's success is that it marked the beginning of fundamental change in the City. His breakthrough in the 1950s was the first concrete evidence that the old order was giving way, and that a system based purely on personal contacts could not survive unless it was at the same time innovative and responsive to merit. But it was only after he had masterminded a bitterly resisted takeover bid for British Aluminium that his voice was heard. The establishment used all its power and resources to defeat him but Warburg turned the tables by gaining allies from outside the City – enlisting the power of the press and appealing direct to British Aluminium's shareholders over the heads of its board and advisers.

His success was not easily forgiven, but it marked the first glimmerings of the dawn of a day when contacts were not everything. Warburg's victory was the first sign that the incestuous contact-based system, which allowed complacency to flourish under the warm blanket of long-term client relationships, was no longer enough and that an American-style transaction-based system where the operator is only as good as his last deal might one day come to the City.

The story of the City since then has been one of a slow but inexorable build-up of pressure to change. Some, like the Rothschilds in 1980 and the Hambros in 1986, have found that the scale of changes required was simply too great and their governing families have divided. Jacob Rothschild split from cousin Evelyn to set up his own financial services group. Rupert Hambro did likewise, leaving cousin Charles.

What made Warburg's act so difficult for the others to follow was that it discarded the things the City held most dear. Warburg's originality – and hence his unpopularity – lay in the way he ignored the conventional practices of the City of London. 'I don't want to do things the way other people do', he wrote in his private journal. 'I have no model. I do things my way.' It was his biggest heresy. For until Warburg reminded the City of its entrepreneurial past, the City wanted people to conform.

This remains the great unanswered question about the City in the closing stages of the twentieth century. If one thing has given the City the capacity to evolve and cope with change down the generations it has been its ability to make newcomers want to become members of the club rather than to break it up. The most militant radical gradually has his edges rounded. Even Warburg ultimately joined the Accepting Houses Committee, and other much

lesser lights change markedly over the years. Northern
accents disappear, mannerisms are cultivated, personal
histories are re-written and the most determined outsider
becomes a clone of the establishment.

In the past the influx was small in proportion to the
numbers already in the City, and those coming in arrived
in a position of weakness rather than strength. The
changes of the 1980s have brought a different style of
immigrant – one who was strong and self-sufficient – and
for the first time this put the establishment on the defen-
sive. But the establishment is nothing if not tenacious and
it remains to be seen whether the newly created firms of
the mid-1980s will develop a genuinely new style of their
own, suited to survival in the modern world, or whether
they will in time revert to the old ways and the old mannerisms of the City, and content themselves with a comfortable and genteel decline. This is one possibility. But in
many ways as likely is the probability that the financial
conglomerates will evolve along American lines and come
to handle what might be termed the volume business and
that there will gradually re-emerge an inner culture, the
old elite, which will once again handle the most prestigious
and most specialised deals. The battle between the old and
the new is certainly not yet over.

3
Who Makes the Rules?

The Bank of England

The art of banking is to have a little capital which can be
lent a large number of times. The art of the banking regulator is to insist that banks have sufficient capital to
support their businesses – so that they do not lend too
much. A bank which over-trades, which lends too much, is
vulnerable to a wave of bad debts. Or it could be forced out
of business by depositors losing confidence and demanding
their money back. Neither happens often in Britain now,
but both are still commonplace in America.

The more frequently a bank lends its capital, the more
money it makes, but the lower is the margin of error. The
need for prudence, therefore, puts a constraint for practical
purposes on how much a bank can lend, and acts as a brake
on its profits. Nevertheless, the Bank of England has it in
its power to release that brake by acting as 'lender of last
resort', which means that, at the end of the day, if a commercial bank really needs money in a hurry, then the Bank
will lend it. Those whom the Bank of England will stand
behind in this way are therefore in a position to trade much
more intensively and to use their capital much more effectively than the banks which do not have such privileges.

This is the basis of the Bank of England's power. First,

the entire banking system has to report to it regularly and in great detail in order to comply with the banking acts. The Bank of England therefore monitors the capital of the banks, their deposits and their lending policies to ensure that all are in balance. If it does not like what it finds, it can ultimately withdraw a bank's licence and put it out of business. More likely, if the offending bank cannot or will not put its house in order, the Bank of England will quietly arrange a takeover, or insist on management changes, as the price for maintaining its recognition. Thus the small private bank, Revson, was taken over by investment trusts managed by the MIM group in 1985, and that same year, in a separate operation, Lord Williams decided to resign as chairman of Henry Ansbacher, and Richard Fenhalls was brought in as chief executive to rebuild its fortunes, after its capital base had been destroyed by an ill-advised US acquisition.

The key to the Bank's day-to-day influence lies, however, not in its big stick but in its ability to show favours. It charges different banks different rates of interest when it acts as lender of last resort. Those whom it charges least are those whom it favours most, namely the members of the Discount Houses Association, and, until the net was widened in 1981, the Accepting Houses Committee. The Bank therefore has the ability to fine-tune the system, to show approval or disapproval, by making life easier and more profitable for those it likes and harder and less profitable for those it dislikes. It does this by relaxing the capital requirements of the discount houses so that they can buy far more Treasury Bills than would normally be considered prudent; or by charging the Accepting Houses a specially low rate of interest when they come to borrow from it. The privileges that go with being a member of the inner circle thus translate directly into profit. It is for this reason, as the chairman of one discount house put it, that when the Bank says jump, you ask how high.[1]

The deregulation of the Stock Exchange, the rapid internationalisation of the banking business, and the increasing overlap between the banking and securities businesses, made this kind of regulation less effective as the 1980s progressed, because it depended on small players whom the Bank could bully, rather than global firms who could treat it with disdain. At the same time, as we shall see in chapter 6, there was a diminishing respect in Whitehall for the Bank of England's advice on monetary policy because, while this had traditionally been the Bank's responsibility, the incoming Thatcher administration of 1979 was heavily monetarist, and insisted that the Treasury build up its own expertise in this area.

The Bank of England thus found itself forced more and more into the role of policeman, and its responsibility for supervision spread to new areas like the swaps market, for example. This was the area of international banking where companies could borrow funds in the country and currency where they were well known and could get the lowest rate of interest, and then swap them into another currency of a country where they were less well known and could therefore not have commanded such a low rate, had they gone directly into the market. The Bank of England here again allowed banks whom it favoured easier conditions of compliance than those it regarded as less acceptable. It monitored the changes at the Stock Exchange by insisting, with government backing, that it have representatives on the Council, and it took on the supervision of the wholesale money markets where it alone could decide who was 'fit and proper' enough to do business.

But it found it faced a problem with the securities markets. In the drafting of legislation leading to the Financial Services Act of 1986, it feared that the government would create a statutory body like the American Securities and Exchange Commission, SEC, a move which it abhorred because it would challenge its own pre-eminence. Yet it did not feel competent to regulate the markets itself – suspecting, perhaps wisely, that there were bound to be some financial failures, and being unwilling to be put in a position where it would have to shoulder the blame. It had, at the time this decision was being taken, suffered a severe mauling in Parliament arising from the failure of Johnson Matthey Bankers in October 1984, and the need to rescue this organisation which, because of the parent company's membership of the gold bullion ring, was very much part of the establishment.

As a compromise, therefore, it acquiesced in the creation of the Securities and Investment Board and ordered the City to do likewise. It prevented the mobilisation of effective opposition by asking the City's most influential group, the chairmen of the banks in the Accepting Houses Committee, to refrain from public criticism of the measure, whatever their private misgivings,[2] on the basis that if they complained they would get something worse. But this was a miscalculation. The Bank misjudged the political mood and the determination even of Conservative politicians, after the embarrassments of Westland and Guinness, to bring a more accountable and visible form of regulation to the City. The SIB that was created was a far more vigorous creature than anyone in the City had foreseen, and the Bank gradually woke up to the fact in 1987 that there was a new force in the City, and a new form of regulation based on written rules and legally enforceable clauses operating alongside and intertwined with the old system of nods and winks. Three hundred years after its founding in 1694, the Bank of England had a serious political challenger for its job as City policeman.

The role of committees

Nevertheless, while the SIB may or may not be the force of the future, the City in the mid-1980s was still very much in the hands of the Bank. And its chosen method of exerting its influence is to rule through committees – one for each designated area of market activity.

The political in-fighting in City committees is every bit as important as the in-fighting in the committees of any political party. The lesson of politics has been that whoever controls the committees controls the party machine and, regardless of what the grass roots may think or want, controls the political process. It is the same, in a no less brutal way, in the City. The work of the City is done in committee. The regulation of the City is rooted in committee. Acceptable behaviour in the City is what the committee feels is acceptable. So control of committees is the key to control of the City.

Two committees, the Discount Houses Committee which governs the firms through which the Bank controls the government debt market, and the Accepting Houses Committee, through which it controls the merchant banks, are the inner core of the City establishment. They set the basic pattern for the system of self-regulation which has guided the City right through to the mid-1980s. Committees are the conduits through which the Bank of England lets its wishes be known. By encouraging the formation of committees and associations for different City activities and then putting pressure on them, the Bank of England disseminates its influence throughout all the different markets. By regulating procedures and setting standards the committee establishes a code of conduct, and cuts down the likelihood of newcomers shaking up the markets with riskily innovative ideas or too vigorous competition.

Following the pattern of the discount market and the Accepting Houses, almost every area of City activity came to have its own committee, with its own rules. There is the Committee of London Clearing Bankers, the Sterling Brokers Association, the Life Offices Association, the Issuing Houses Association – no activity is too large or too small to be governed in this way. A typical committee set the standards it wanted for its sector of activity. It controlled membership by deciding whom it would admit to the association. It recommended rates of commission. It created common services for use only by approved committee members. No reason was given to those whom it chose to exclude, but inevitably these were organisations which appeared to be too threatening or too powerful for the existing members to want to compete with them. On most occasions, too, the committee system meant that foreign firms were also barred from competing in the City's most lucrative markets. The US banking group, Citicorp, was barred right up to the 1980s from membership of the Committee of London Clearing Bankers, because the British banks wanted to keep it out of the High Street. Elsewhere, no foreign firm was ever admitted to the gold bullion ring or the Accepting Houses Committee. It was the committee's view, endorsed by the Bank of England, that business would be done on terms acceptable to those already in the market or it would not be done at all. The committee was the old boy network, backed by the power of the establishment.

There were, of course, plus points to compensate in efficiency for what was in effect a gross restraint of competition. First, the committee structure acted as an effective brake on possible wrongdoers, and the voluntary nature of the 'legislation' made its justice flexible and fast moving. But it was rough justice – nothing was written down, so nothing was ever official or available to be challenged. Participants in the market had to act in the spirit of the club, rather than to follow the letter of the law. This meant that the London markets could be flexible and respond to the changing patterns of finance in a way which the much more legalistic systems of Wall Street and Tokyo found more difficult. But it also meant that they could featherbed and exploit monopolies, without fear of innovation or excessive disturbance in their market. So the efficiency gains were decidedly mixed.

The codes of conduct are supposedly voluntary, as is membership of the association. But the reality is rather more brutal. A non-member cannot do business because other City firms will not deal with it. In this way the committee system makes it possible for each branch of the City to operate a closed shop against newcomers, and to eliminate competition with a rigidity and effectiveness which would be the envy of any trade union leader.

The gilts market

As the financial markets are in a continual state of flux, there is a need from time to time for new committees to be formed to regulate new activities. The British gilt-edged market – the market dealing in government securities – is a case in point. Though superficially efficient at raising money cheaply for the government, the growth in the number of firms operating in the market had not kept pace with the vast increase in the amount of capital needing to be raised, and the Bank of England in the 1980s decided on wholesale reform, to recast the market along American lines.

Thoughout much of 1985 the Bank developed its plans. Under the old system of issuing stock two major jobbing firms, Akroyd and Smithers and Wedd Durlacher, had acted in cosy harmony with a Bank representative, the senior partner of Mullens, who was known as the Government Broker. In the wider international financial market of the 1980s, it was decided to replace this system by an open competitive market of 29 firms, many of them American and several others of continental European origin. There was no magic in the figure of 29; the Bank said that all whom it considered fit and proper could take part. Significantly, no Japanese houses participated initially; they held back rather than risk rejection, believing, probably correctly, that the lack of freedom given to UK firms in Tokyo would count against them here.[3]

To control the conduct of the market, the Bank naturally wanted a committee, but because of the foreign involvement, membership had, unusually, to include foreign-owned firms. And the foreign firms – realising that in the City he who controls the committee controls the conduct of the market – were anxious to participate. The Bank therefore co-opted a team of would-be practitioners in the market, selecting them so as to provide a cross-section of the 29 who were to be involved, but ensuring at the same time that, in spite of the presence of one or two Americans, the committee was heavily slanted towards British houses, and within that towards the most establishment-minded of them.

The Bank provided a secretary, premises and back up services for the committee in its early days while it drafted detailed rules and regulations for the market. In this way it was kept fully informed about how things were progressing, without having to be reduced to asking for information – an act which would have been considered demeaning, if not vulgar. Opposition was dealt with along the way by asking critics to 'present a paper', thereby drawing their sting. Complaints were either satisfactorily dealt with, or

complainants bowed to the inevitable. But the exercise was
conducted with sufficient tact for the opposition never to be
allowed to coalesce and become either vocal or united.

Once satisfactory rules were in place and the prepara-
tory work completed, the Bank then decided its Committee
was ready for independent life. The permanent committee
was to have fewer members than the co-opted one, so an
election was necessary. Equally inevitably the bulk, if not
all, of the candidates for the new committee were those
whom the Bank had co-opted on to the interim committee.

In the City the results were seen as a triumph for the
Bank. Top of the poll came George Nissen of Morgan Gren-
fell/Pember and Boyle, a member of the Stock Exchange
Council and undoubtedly the most establishment candidate on the ticket. The next slots were filled by representatives from the two firms which had run the market in the
past – from Wedd and from Akroyd, part of the Warburg
securities group which now also controlled Mullens. John
Hutchinson, the candidate from Merrill Lynch, the American house most feared by the British because of its awe-
some financial power, came second from the bottom. The
elections successfully legitimised the committee in the
eyes of the membership, and equally successfully ensured
that the running of the market in its formative years
would be in the hands of those in whom the Bank of
England has confidence. A new area of City activity had
been created, and brought smoothly under the wing of the
Bank.

The Takeover Panel

The apotheosis of the committee structure was the Takeover Panel, which was created in 1969. The City was at the
time engaged in one of its periodic bouts of merger fever,
and some of the tactics used, by Cazenove among others,
had led to adverse comment in Parliament and the press.
The Bank of England, as ever anxious to head off any
outside interference and 'to preserve the City's good name',

prompted those concerned with takeover activity – primarily the leading merchant banks – to set up a panel which would act as a neutral arbiter. The Panel, appropriately enough, was made up of the chairmen of the relevant leading City committees – the Unit Trust Association, the Accepting Houses Committee, the Issuing Houses Association, the Investment Trust Association and so on – and they in turn appointed a small executive, with a rotating staff of people drawn from the Accepting Houses inner core of the merchant banks and law firms.

As long as the City continued to be a cosy club in which all the members were prepared to abide by club rules, the Panel was a success. From its creation at the end of the 1960s right through to the mid-1980s, it protected shareholders in UK public companies from most of the excesses which disfigured the American markets at that time, by maintaining as its guiding principle that all shareholders in a company had to be treated equally. It was impossible therefore for company managements to pay 'greenmail'[4] and destroy the financial health of their companies to preserve their own positions, as happened in the United States.

Those benefits were not without their costs, however, though characteristically these fell on companies and individuals outside the City rather than on their advisers within the Square Mile. If a company decided to ignore the findings of the Panel, then the Bank of England, on the Panel's behalf, could request that the City institutions withdraw their facilities from that company. Not only would a company thus treated lose its stock market quote and its advisers, but the banks which had lent it money would not renew the loans when they came up for review, an action which would effectively bankrupt the company. Nor was this 'nuclear deterrent' simply for show. There were occasions when companies were directly threatened with its use, as in the case of Ashbourne Investments in the 1970s.[5] Given that the system was non-statutory, and that there was then no legal redress against the Panel's rulings, it was an arbitrary and sometimes harsh system.

Nevertheless, the Panel appeared to keep the system

much cleaner than it was in America. It had its critics, mainly on account of its arbitrariness and inconsistency, which arose because being fair sometimes meant changing its mind as a bid developed in the light of new information. Americans in particular yearned for a fixed set of rules so that they knew what they could and could not do. The absence of such rules inhibited the growth of London as an international share-dealing centre according to some people, because foreign investors were reluctant to put in money when the rules of the game might suddenly change to their disadvantage.[6] The skill of the British merchant banks in moulding Panel verdicts to their wishes was one major reason why they could hope to maintain an edge over firms such as Goldman Sachs, who found it difficult to understand how to push the rules to the limit in the interests of their clients when the interpretation of how far to push the rules depended on who was doing the pushing.[7]

The basic integrity of the system was hinted at by the fact that leading US stock market figures like the later disgraced insider trader Ivan Boesky could complain at 'rules which change depending on what the regulators had for breakfast',[8] but also at its unfairness about which the leading Australian businessman John Elliot was even more scathing. When his company Elders IXL tried to bid for Allied Lyons in 1985–6 he insisted that his advisers, merchant bank Hill Samuel, refer to the Panel not by its proper name but as the New York Yacht Club. At the time the NYYC was notorious for holding on to the America's Cup for more than a century by judiciously changing the rules every time a challenger threatened to win.[9]

At bottom, the main criticism was that the Panel was the creature of the City establishment, and was there to preserve the power and influence of the inner circle of banks and brokers. Time and again it allowed established City names to use tactics which were barred to less well connected houses. As a result, bidders backed by an establishment firm had a much greater chance of winning in any contested bid battle. Thus the takeovers of the mid-1980s saw the same few firms, Morgan Grenfell, Kleinwort, Hill Samuel and Warburg, cropping up time and time again, and also saw aggressive bidders like Guinness and Ward White sever long-held relationships to forge new ones with the inner group. This in turn allowed them to charge much higher fees for their services. If a company wanted to win – like Guinness for Bells, or Dixons for Curry's – it was a price it had to pay.

The complaints from non-establishment figures of discrimination are legion, though most complain only in private because they do not want to be black-balled – shunned by the inner core of institutions. But some rows become public, as for example in 1986 when the establishment-backed Stewart Goldsmith's unquoted Fredericks Place Group and the very non-establishment Tony Cole of Bestwood joined battle for control of the Country Gentlemen's Association. Bestwood's initial complaint was that the Panel permitted a valuation of Frederick's Place Group shares to be carried in the offer document, which in turn allowed the company to declare that its bid – a share exchange – was worth substantially more than the rival offer from Bestwood. The point of the grievance was that the Frederick's Place shares were then unquoted and therefore their value could only be guessed at. The Panel accepted the valuation because it came from Cazenove, whereas it would never have accepted a guess prepared by a less well connected house.

Later the bid was increased – an action which automatically decreased the intrinsic worth of the bidder's shares, because more now stood to be issued to acquire an unchanged amount of assets. This might have caused a downward revision in Cazenove's estimate of the notional market price. But in fact the price remained the same, thus enhancing the value of Cazenove's client's bid and giving the client a significant competitive advantage in a battle it was indeed eventually to win.

Such freedom of manoeuvre gave the big houses significant competitive advantage, when spread across the market as a whole, and was a key factor in allowing them to maintain their grip on activity in the City. Outsiders like Elliot, or Robert Maxwell the publisher, and even major companies like Imperial Group all found they could do nothing when a Panel decision went against them, because

no financial adviser would ever associate himself with a
challenge to the Panel's authority. Imperial Group, when
fighting an ultimately successful takeover bid from Hanson Trust, was enraged when the Panel decided to ban
advertising during bid battles. It wanted to take the Panel
to the European Court, but its merchant bank adviser
threatened to resign rather than support a challenge to the
Panel.[10] Some years earlier lawyer Stanley Berwin sought
to challenge the Panel over the rough treatment he considered was meted out by the Sotheby's board to two US
bidders, Messrs Cogan and Swid. Again, the suggestion led
to the threatened resignation of the bidder's advisers.[11]

The Panel proved to be a major bulwark of the City
establishment for over fifteen years, and it was only in the
mid-1980s that its authority was finally challenged. The
threat came from the established merchant banks who,
consciously or unconsciously, began to imitate the American houses then starting to set up corporate finance departments in London, and became more and more aggressive in search of success in takeovers, and less and less
mindful of the restraints imposed by club membership.
Morgan Grenfell became adept at blunting the Panel's will
by bogging it down in detail. Hill Samuel, acting with
Cazenove, censured for breaching Panel rules in the AE
battle, showed by its lack of public contrition that the
censure carried little sting.

Then, in early 1987, Pru Bache, an American house
headed by an ex-Kleinwort Benson man, took the Panel to
the Court of Appeal, and secured the judgement that Panel
rulings could ultimately be challenged in Court. It was the
beginning of the end. The consensus had broken down
because the City was no longer a club, and could no longer
be run on club rules. During its fifteen-year life, the Panel
had served the club well, and ensured the prosperity of a
whole generation of the merchant banking elite. But after
the Pru Bache verdict, and its perceived shortcomings over
Guinness, it seemed it could survive in the future only
under the wing and with the legal backing of the SIB.

Investment Protection Committees

Other brakes on the activity of City firms, rivalling the
Takeover Panel in power but much less publicly accountable, are the investment protection committees. These are
standing committees of the investing institutions – the
pension funds, the insurance companies and the investment trusts – which rarely make public pronouncements or
issue public documents, though some are occasionally
leaked. For many years they never even admitted who sat
on their various committees.

They wield tremendous power because they decide, on
behalf of the fund managers in their respective groups,
whether to support a company's fund-raising exercise, a
takeover bid, a share option scheme, or even the continuation in office of its current board. They therefore hold in
their power the success or failure of a takeover bid, for
while they rarely recommend to fellow investment managers which way they should vote on such an issue, they are
tenacious in their insistence that the terms should have a
cash alternative and should avoid the issue of securities of
uncertain value. As such, they are a definite brake on the
freedom of manoeuvre of merchant banks. They also insist
that the City fund managers get their share of the commissions in takeover bids, by refusing to support bids or rights
issues where there is no underwriting, though there has
been some mellowing after their demands earned them a
rebuke from the Bank of England.[12] Such commissions
have added massively to the costs of a bid; of the £100
million fees Guinness paid in bidding for Argyll, for instance, four-fifths were underwriting charges.

The basic motivation of investment protection committees was, of course, selfish. The typical procedure was to
form an *ad hoc* working party to thrash out behind closed
doors a common line on anything innovative or controversial. This greatly upset company chairmen like Alec Monk
of Dee Corporation who objected, not to the committees'
existence as such, but to the fact that they took far-

reaching decisions against which the company concerned had no appeal, and of whose activities it was frequently not made aware.[16] He argued that the activities of such committees served to protect the interests of the fund managers in the City, at the expense of the companies which had to use the system, and whose freedom for manoeuvre and innovation in their financing techniques was circumscribed and their costs increased.

Another weakness was that they were sometimes inconsistent, particularly once they had to operate in the public arena. In early 1987 the Burton Group directors tried to secure shareholder approval for a share option package which, if certain performance targets were met, would have yielded them massive benefits. Warburg, the merchant bank advising Burton, thought it had piloted the scheme safely through even before it was made public, by conducting secret negotiations with the Investment Protection Committee for the insurance industry. But when the proposal became public knowledge, and generated criticism because of its apparently excessive generosity, the institutional investors took fright and reneged on their private promises. The scheme had to be significantly watered down before it was safe to put it to the vote of the mass of shareholders.

Investment Protection Committees are part of the concealed fabric of the City, which ensures that the voice of fund managers is heard on the issues of the day and that companies of which the system disapproves are brought to heel. But as the name implies, it is a negative form of control; the committees are much better at resisting what they do not like, than at coming up with constructive ideas for change.

To the Bank of England's chagrin, they are poor at using their power constructively to put pressure on the managements of companies which fail to perform well,[14] though there are exceptions; Turner and Newall chief Sir Francis Tombs was appointed as a result of IPC behind-the-scenes pressure on the old board. In general, however, the dislike of public confrontation has meant that British managements were not galvanised as much as they ought to have

been by their big City shareholders. The existence of the
committees in many ways has thus served to reduce shareholder pressure to the lowest common denominator. They
stopped individual fund managers criticising managements because the form was for such complaints to be
funnelled through an IPC. But usually the IPC could only
agree to do nothing, and as a result second-rate managements were allowed to continue in office until ultimately
removed by bankruptcy or a takeover bid.

The new order

The old committee-based system of regulation broke down
because, as the City expanded and became international,
its practitioners no longer came from the same background. The changing nature of the Accepting Houses
Committee shows this dramatically. The 1960s Accepting
House Committee was redolent with familiar names. It
contained a Baring, a Kleinwort, a Rothschild, a Seligman,
a Hambro and a Brandt. There were five Lords, and others
with high honours. Almost all were members of the original banking families. All went to Eton or one of the top-
flight public schools.

In the 1980s the picture changed, however. Only five of
its members had been to Eton, and four did not attend
public school at all. Several had not even had a traditional
city career. Singer and Friedlander's Anthony Solomons,
though he went to Oundle, trained as an accountant not a
banker. Malcolm Wilcox was an 'NCO' who worked his way
up through the ranks to become chief general manager of
Midland Bank before retiring and moving to Rea Brothers.
Albert Frost did likewise, working his way up through one
of the largest industrial companies to become finance
director of ICI, and after his retirement becoming connected with Guinness Mahon. Staffan Gadd of Montagu
and Winifried Bischoff of Schroders were both born and
educated abroad.

Changes in the committees were replicated in the type of
people working in the City as a whole. The traditional City
was one where the inner circle of merchant banks, discount

houses, the Stock Exchange and insurance companies called the tune. The new City was different. Its composition is
best illustrated by the membership of the Capital Markets
Committee, a body set up in 1983 by the Governor of the
Bank of England to advise him on the changes which were
then beginning to take place. Traditionally, when the Governor, by custom and practice the City's spokesman,
wanted to sound out the City's views he would talk to the
organisations listed above. The creation of the Capital
Markets Committee was recognition that that was no longer good enough.

The Capital Markets Committee came into existence,
according to the press release of the time 'to act as a focal
point within the City for views concerning current issues
and future developments including company law matters,
which affect the domestic and international capital markets of the City'. The fourteen members of the Committee
in February 1985 were as follows:

Nicholas Baring, chairman. Managing director, Baring
    Brothers. Occupation: merchant banker.
Ronald Artus, Group chief investment manager, Pruden-
    tial Corporation. Occupation: investment manage-
    ment.
Peter Gerrard, Senior partner, White Lovell and King.
    Occupation: solicitor.
John Gunn, Chief executive, Exco International. Occupa-
    tion: money broker.
David Leroy Lewis, Deputy Chairman, Touche Remnant.
    Occupation: investment trust manager.
Richard Lloyd, Deputy Chairman and chief executive, Hill
    Samuel. Occupation: merchant banker.
Ralph Quartano, Chief executive, Postel Investment Man-
    agement. Occupation: pension fund manager.
John Quinton, Deputy Chairman, Barclays Bank. Occupa-
    tion: commercial banker.
Edward Ray, Partner, Spicer and Pegler. Occupation: char-
    tered accountant.
John Robertson, Senior partner, Wedd Durlacher. Occupa-
    tion: stock jobber.

William Stuttaford, Chairman, Framlington Group.
  Occupation: fund manager.
Richard Sykes. Occupation: Queens Counsel, specialising
  in company law.
Richard Westmacott, Chairman, Hoare Govett. Occupa-
  tion: stockbroker.
Nicholas Wilson, partner, Slaughter and May. Occupation:
  solicitor.

The members of this committee were the new, not the old
City. When compared with the hierarchy of the Accepting
Houses, they appeared to show that wealth and power have
become much more widely dispersed and are no longer the
privilege of a small caste.

That is not to say, however, that the committee reflected
all the changes, for the first and most obvious omission is
any member representing a non-British firm. The crucially
important Eurodollar markets, which dwarf the rest of the
London capital markets, are unrepresented. The committee shows that professionals with qualifications are now
evenly mixed with the old family firms of the City, and
where Etonians and Oxbridge still predominate it is very
much because they hold their positions on merit. Today's
markets have become too competitive for it to be otherwise.

Thus the committee was much more 'cloth cap' than any
of its predecessors. At one stage it included Hugh Jenkins,
a Llanelli grammar school boy, who did National Service
in the Royal Artillery but became head of investment management at the Coal Board Superannuation Fund. Ron
Artus worked his way up to become chief investment manager for the Prudential. Likewise John Quinton, who has
come up through the ranks to become the first non-family
head of Barclays, and Eddie Ray, who is senior partner of
chartered accountants Spicer and Pegler. One was educated at state school in Norwich, the other in Holloway,
North London. Add in two solicitors and a barrister, a
senior figure from Wedd Durlacher, the jobbers, two stockbrokers, one investment trust representative, and two
bankers, one from Hill Samuel and the other, the chairman
of the committee, Sir Nicholas Baring, and it provides a

much clearer picture of where power lies and how it is
spread in the still British-controlled City of today.

It rests in a coalition of lawyers and accountants, bankers and brokers, fund managers and institutional investors. Some are old, some are new but they represent a quite
clear diversification of skills and a movement away from
traditional City interests.

Statutory regulation

If time and change made the collapse of the old system
inevitable, it will have been hastened by some ham-fisted
work by the Bank of England which led to the creation of a
new regulatory body, whose powers derive directly from an
Act of Parliament – the Securities and Investments Board
created by the Financial Services Act of 1986.

This problem for the Bank had its origins in the early
1980s when two commodity trading houses, Norton Warburg and ML Doxford, collapsed within a few months of
each other with the loss of several million pounds of clients'
money. Ironically, among those clients was the Bank of
England pension fund. This, plus the fact that dealing
houses of this nature did not come under the wing of the
Bank of England but were licensed directly by the Department of Trade and Industry, caused an outburst of indignation in Threadneedle Street and led the Bank – always
keen to score points off its rivals in Whitehall – to lobby
vigorously for such firms to be effectively regulated.

This backfired badly, however, when the Government
responded by asking Professor Jim Gower of the City University to conduct a one-man inquiry and to prepare a
report with recommendations on how to update the laws on
investor protection. Unfortunately for the City, Professor
Gower had been a client of a stockbroking firm, Hedder-
wick, which had gone out of business just a few months
previously. His money was returned as was that of all
members of the public by payments out of the Stock Exchange compensation fund. But the first- hand experience
of the uncertainties of the investment world had certainly
heightened Professor Gower's appreciation of the task in

hand, and he produced a report[15] which was much more comprehensive and fundamental in its call for reforms than perhaps anyone had expected at the outset.

The legislation based on his report, the 1986 Financial Services Act, imposed a comprehensive system of regulation which on paper at least went far beyond anything the City had looked for. The most fundamental change was the introduction of a whole new structure of regulation, with the guiding principle that all organisations offering investment services to the public had to be authorised by the Secretary of State for Trade and Industry. This was undoubtedly regulation by statute. The Act also gave the Minister power to delegate this regulatory function to approved voluntary bodies accountable to him, on the basis that these would be more likely to have the degree of detailed expertise needed to do the job effectively. This led to the creation of the Securities and Investments Board as the vehicle to take on board the Minister's powers day to day. Its first chairman, Sir Kenneth Berrill, was appointed jointly by the Secretary of State for Trade and Industry in consultation with the Governor of the Bank of England.

When the idea of a new regulatory board for the growing securities and investments industry was being sold to the City, it was stressed that its creation would serve to preserve and enhance the self-regulation which, as we have seen, was the essence of City policing. But in 1987, in the wake of the Guinness scandal which sent the politicians scuttling for scapegoats, those statements have been rapidly set on one side and another aspect of the SIB is now being stressed. The SIB emphasised the steel fist beneath the velvet glove by seeking to make its writ run to the very heart of the system and to draft rules with the force of law for every activity. It was then seen to have virtually all the powers of, and promises to be every bit as tough as, the American Securities and Exchange Commission, the supervisory model which so many politicians have seen as a panacea for all regulatory problems.

No one has been more to the fore in promoting this changed perception of the SIB than its Chairman, who early in 1987 described the nature of the system in the following uncompromising terms: 'We went for and we have a statutory system'. The powers of the SIB are 'a very tough bunch of powers'.[16] It derives its powers directly from the Financial Services Act and began but producing two large volumes of rule books, both of which have the full force of law. 'Every single word of them is a statutory declaration', according to Berrill. But it is not only the SIB rules which will have the force of law. This also extends to the rules and regulations of the self-regulatory organisations which the SIB ultimately recognised. Their rules had to obtain SIB approval before the SIB would agree to delegate to them the day-to-day work of regulating the market place, and this act of recognition makes their rules statutory.

In Sir Kenneth's words, the City is no longer 'a free for all' where 'you look after yourself according to a code of honour or conduct. It is a tough regulatory system.' Indeed, he dismissed the very phrase self-regulatory organisations as an 'interesting carrying on of an expression which I don't think is valid any more'. They are self-regulating in the sense that people join them and they elect their own councils. But the form of their councils, committees and organisation is very carefully constrained. They regulate themselves, but within very carefully imposed rules and regulations, set down under statute.

This is exactly the American system. The Securities and Exchange Commission does not run any exchanges. It relies on the New York Stock Exchange to do the actual regulation. Right across the United States, it works through what London would call self-regulating organisations.

The elite re-emerges

The months following the passing of the Financial Services Act and the creation of the Securities and Investments Board thus heralded a revolution in the way the City was regulated. But if it was the intention of the regulators to change the face of City regulation they failed to allow for the capacity of the City establishment to regenerate itself.

Even in the early days of the new system, at its most formative stage, it was possible to detect signs of establishment takeover to protect the interests of the elite. The SIB had decided to delegate its regulatory powers to half a dozen bodies, each covering a sphere of City activity, and the practitioners in each sphere had to elect their officials and pay for the regulation of their own membership. Six of these were planned, but even before they became properly functional, they were dividing along class lines. The upper-crust City firms gravitated to one kind of self-regulatory body and excluded those of whom they did not approve; the lower orders became members of an altogether less exclusive club.

The banks' decision on which organisation to join illustrated this point. There is no self-regulatory organisation exclusively for banks, because their banking activities are supervised by the Bank of England. However, they need to register with an SRO for their other, non-banking, activities. The chief executive of the Investment Management Regulatory Organisation, IMRO, John Morgan, expressed delight that the clearing banks were almost certain to choose his organisation as their major self-regulatory body, though they could equally well have become members of Fimbra, the organisation designed to cover financial inter-mediaries and investment managers. 'This is a very strong endorsement of IMRO as a dominant force in certain parts of the City', he said.[17] As far as the members were concerned, they clearly wanted to join an organisation which they felt reflected their status and image. 'In theory both IMRO and Fimbra would serve, but our bias is towards IMRO because we are talking to people we understand. Some organisations are easier to work with than others, and it often comes down to a question of personalities', one banker commented.[18] Clearly IMRO thinks of itself as a cut above Fimbra, and members of IMRO are more up-market than members of other SROs. The elitism is re-establishing itself.

The SROs also behave like a club, rejecting members not necessarily because they fail to meet the established criteria, but because they are regarded as not suitable.

LHW Futures is a controversial commodities broker whose application in 1986 for membership of the Association of Futures Brokers and Dealers was turned down. It took the matter to appeal and Mr J. H. Davis, vice-chairman of Lloyds Bank, was appointed by the Governor of the Bank of England in December 1986 to look into the matter.

Though he did not overturn the verdict, Mr Davis sharply criticised the AFBD for the way in which the decision was reached.[19] He wrote in his judgement:

> There may have been an inclination both in the Executive and in the Council to pre-judge the issue because of LHW's unfavourable reputation . . . . Insufficient inquiry was made both by Council and by the Executive into any measures which the new Managing Director might have brought in . . . Both Council and Executive were too concerned to observe the letter of AFBD's Articles of Association and Rules rather than the spirit which I consider would have been justified in the circumstances.

If members are to be held financially responsible for the actions of their fellow club members as well as their own, then it is only natural that they should seek to vet strictly who is in the club with them. Nevertheless, it does not bode well for City regulation that the SROs should evolve into a two-tier system with the elite clustered and secure in their up-market self-regulatory organisations, while the others are condemned to membership of one or more vast, under-financed and unwieldy bodies. It need hardly be added that it will be to the body where the resources are the scarcest, and the supervision spread most thin, that those most in need of regulation will gravitate. And that, if anything, will confirm the establishment in its view that it is right to be elitist.

Conclusion

It remains to be seen whether the new system will have the necessary teeth. The problem in the City with the Guinness affair and all the other scandals which have been kept under wraps has never been a lack of rules; it has been the unwillingness of those with the power to enforce them against their own kind. So there has always been two-tier justice in the City. Whether something was permitted or not depended on who was doing the rule-breaking.

On one level, the creation of the SIB appeared to be a defeat for the City because a new watchdog had been created and the City, via the Governor of the Bank of England, had only a muted and secondary voice in the selection of its chairman. Moreover, the main objective of the Bank of England was to avoid the creation of a statutory body directly responsible for the financial markets – a Securities and Exchange Commission on the American model – because this would have brought the law directly into the City and would have spelled the end of self-regulation.

So the Bank failed in its primary task. But underneath the SIB are a series of Self-Regulatory Organisations. Though these are a new feature of City life, they are effectively the old committees and associations welded into larger units, each with the responsibility to monitor the behaviour of City firms and individuals within designated areas of activity. The people in charge of the new SROs are the people who had been in charge of the old committees, and they brought with them their old beliefs and customs.

The SROs are more open than the old committees, and they have had to be more professional in the way they regulate the markets, by preparing and publishing detailed rules on the way members should conduct their business. They are substantially more costly to run. And they also have to embrace all members of the City with a legitimate right to do business there, rather than try to keep foreign firms out simply because they are foreign. But the type of person who came forward for committee work in the old City is the same type who is involved in the new, and the attitudes of the people who run the committees have not changed.

On top of that they also have legal immunity, and cannot be sued for what they do in the way of regulation. This means that they retain those essential rights which were the hallmark of the old committee system – the power to ban someone or some firm from conducting business because, in the eyes of his fellow practitioners in the market, he is not a fit and proper person. It is too early to write off the new system, but it is also too early to say that the old one is dead. It could well be a case of 'plus ça change, plus c'est la même chose.'

4
Missed Opportunities

The great change taking place in the financial markets is that the world is moving towards becoming one unified global market, which means that investors and companies wanting to raise money are no longer confined to doing their business in their domestic markets. Instead, they can scour the world looking for the best deal, and the financial centres, which had grown accustomed to being local monopolies, have suddenly found themselves facing cut-throat competition.

The major financial markets in the mid-1980s were in New York, Tokyo and London. Of these three, London was the smallest in size in securities trading but was still the world leader in offshore banking, insurance and foreign-exchange dealing. And it had a priceless advantage over the others, because it was in the middle time zone which linked the other two. London is the only market where it is possible to talk to Tokyo in the early morning and Wall Street in the afternoon, and is therefore the crucially strategic link in the chain of global trading.

Dealers will not work 24 hours a day in New York or Tokyo, but will prefer to pass their trading positions round the world with the sun, towards whichever market is about to open as they close. London will therefore remain one of the world's big three financial centres because of this acci-

dent of geography, almost regardless of what happens to
the domestic British institutions. It may be that the problems of risk control caused by passing on the actual trading
book will lead to this management function being concentrated in the time zone where the organisation is head-
quartered and where people will be forced to work shifts.[1]
But that would make little difference to London. The sales
and research operations for Europe would still have to be
based there.

What came to be realised in the early 1980s, however,
was that, in the absence of major and sweeping reform, the
British firms would be too small to survive in this global
pool and London would soon be dominated by foreign,
mainly American, organisations. These would be almost
fully staffed by British personnel; but the top jobs would be
reserved for Americans. As the decade progressed, the sudden arrival of the Japanese on the world financial scene, as
that country became a massive exporter of capital, showed
just how urgent the foreign threat had become.

The Eurobond market

There was already a precedent for foreign domination in
the Eurobond market, the market for company and government borrowing which grew up in the 25 years from 1960
to become the largest bond market in the world – bigger
even than that of the domestic United States. The money
which was lent in this market came from every country in
the world, and was in virtually every currency, though
dollars, yen and Deutschmarks came to dominate it.[2] And
though there was no physical market place, its hub was
London. The reasons for this were two-fold. First, it was a
British invention – if German-born Siegmund Warburg
can be counted as British. Secondly, London did not have
laws restricting the rates of interest which could be paid on
deposits, and other laws separating banking activity from
underwriting and issuing activity in the securities and
bonds markets, both of which existed in the United States.

Nevertheless, the combination of aversion to risk and
unfamiliarity with the new techniques meant that the

British banks failed to dominate the Eurobond markets as they should have done. Table 4.1 illustrates just how far adrift the British were.

Table 4.1 The leading Eurobond houses 1986

Rank	Bank	Amount $m.	No. of issues	Market Share %	Nationality
1 (1)	Credit Suisse First Boston	20,428.10	108	11.20	Swiss/US
2 (8)	Nomura Securities	14,321.60	129	7.85	Japanese
3 (5)	Deutsche Bank	12,156.10	92	6.66	German
4 (3)	Morgan Guaranty	9,821.74	64	5.38	US
5 (12)	Daiwa Securities	8,779.09	87	4.81	Japanese
6 (6)	Morgan Stanley International	8,764.36	73	4.80	US
7 (4)	Salomon Brothers	8,362.25	55	4.58	US
8 (10)	Banque Paribas	6,779.81	67	3.72	French
9 (2)	Merrill Lynch Capital Markets	5,945.45	40	3.26	US
10 (25)	Nikko Securities	5,085.18	54	2.79	Japanese
11 (9)	Union Bank of Switzerland	4,811.71	46	2.64	Swiss
12 (20)	Yamaichi Securities	4,358.39	59	2.39	Japanese
13 (15)	Shearson Lehman Brothers Int	4,122.48	23	2.25	US
14 (7)	Goldman Sachs International	3,654.68	23	2.00	US
15 (21)	Société Générale	3,090.89	27	1.69	French

1985 ranking in brackets
Source: *Euromoney Annual Financing Report*, March 1987. The leading bookrunners.

The Eurobond markets have many subdivisions and specialities, but *Euromoney*, the specialist magazine which covers these markets, considers that the best overall guide to performance is the 'Bookrunners' table, reproduced as Table 4.1. Bookrunning consists not only of floating an issue but also of managing the sale and purchase of securities afterwards, and is therefore a comprehensive guide to the overall strength of a firm.

The Americans have the largest number of firms in the top fifteen, the number one firm, Crédit Suisse First Boston, being of American-Swiss parentage with the Americans having the larger interest. The Japanese houses number just four against the Americans six and a half, but whereas the Japanese have all dramatically improved position, the American houses have, with the exception of Shearson and CSFB, lost ground. The European involvement in the market consists of the German Deutsche Bank in third position, Union Bank of Switzerland at 11, and two French banks at 8 and 15. No British bank figured in the top 15 bookrunners, in spite of the fact that the market is based in London.

There was no one reason why the British banks functioned so poorly in the Eurobond market, but a variety of contributory factors. First, because the market was originally denominated in dollars, and was less restricted and regulated than markets within the continental United States, it was immediately of interest to American banks and American companies. It was less interesting to British banks and British companies, because rigid exchange control up to 1979 effectively prevented most British companies from making use of it.

Another difference was the absence of a tradition of bond markets in Britain because companies relied heavily on bank finance. There was a strong tradition in the United States, however, so inevitably the techniques of the market and the way issues were managed and sold derived from the American rather than the British experience, thereby again giving the Americans a competitive edge.

But the main reason why the British lost out was that the market demanded a willingness to take big risks, because the profits were to be made by buying an issue from a company and then trying to sell it to a large number of investors at a fractionally higher price. British merchant banks were unused to taking such risks and did not have enough capital to take the chance that they might lose heavily the first few times they tried. So, muttering all the while that the business was too competitive to be profitable, they allowed the cuckoos to take over the nest.

The necessary skills did not exist in the British organisations. American issuing techniques lay a great deal of emphasis on the ability to distribute securities over a wide area, whereas the British market is tightly concentrated in the hands of a few hundred institutional fund managers.

The British merchant banks whose job it is to organise capital-raising exercises on behalf of clients could not use the Euromarkets because they had no skill in distributing securities. And the British stockbrokers who had the skill did not have the capital or the awareness to participate in the market. Moreover, to have moved heavily into corporate finance would have been seen as treading too much on the toes of the merchant banks, and would probably have brought a lecture from the Bank of England on the merits of sticking to their own business.

The foreign banks operating in the market were heavily staffed by British nationals, which proved that on an individual level the trading skills and the innovation and adaptability existed in the City. The Euromarkets were thus an opportunity which fell between the two stools of merchant banking and broking institutions. On an individual level, they yielded great benefits to the people who moved into them. The failure of the British to participate was primarily a failure of the organisations and structures to adapt, a failure to change the compartmentalisation of the British single-capacity system. But it was also a failure of its individual members, who in the cosy climate of the City were not culturally attuned to question the existing structures and organisations and force them to adapt.

The takeover of Lloyd's

The Eurobond market was not the only example of what the Americans could achieve if allowed free rein in the City. The Lloyd's insurance market provides another warning. Up to 1980 the Council of Lloyd's exercised one of those unwritten rules, typical of the City, which prevented an American firm taking over a Lloyd's broker. But the rule proved impossible to sustain once the American market became the major source of business for Lloyd's and the Americans were no longer prepared to put up with being treated as second-class citizens. Once the rule was relaxed, the result was dramatic. First, Marsh and McLennan, the world's biggest insurance broker, bid for CT Bowring. Within months Alexander and Alexander, the

second largest American broker, had bought Alexander
Howden. And in 1985 the largest Lloyd's broker of all,
Sedgwick, did a deal with an American broker, which left
the Transamerica Corporation as the largest shareholder
in the firm. Thus within three years the insurance brokers
who between them dominated the flow of business into the
Lloyd's market came under American control. Only the
specialist underwriters who gave the market its expertise
and flair but who had no need of capital or connections
remained independent.

All change in the City

By the early 1980s, the City was known for its narrow
streets, impressive Victorian buildings, and a way of doing
business which had fallen out of step with modern times.
The Americans, in particular, were out of patience with its
cottage-industry approach which was characterised by
strict separation between different financial activities.
Merchant banks – the aristocrats – financed international
trade, managed portfolios and structured corporate finance
deals. Brokers retailed stocks and shares to investors.
Jobbers acted as wholesalers of shares in the stock market.
Discount houses bought and sold money market instruments on behalf of the big High Street commercial banks.
Not only did a firm not compete outside its designated
area, but even within disciplines there was a network of
cosy cartels and informal associations which ensured that,
with co-operation, each could get its share of the business,
while making sure that no one ever rocked the competitive
boat too vigorously.

From the liveried doorman at the portals of the Bank of
England to some of the best-known names on the polished
brass plates in the world of banking, everybody made a
living. Nor did they have to be British, though, as we have
seen, the welcome to outsiders could be cool to begin with.
None of the major merchant banks – the Rothschilds,
Hambros, Barings, Schroders – was originally British.
Nevertheless, their existence proved that one of the City's
unsung skills has been to provide an ultimately liberal

haven for persecuted foreigners and to benefit by absorbing their skills and moulding them into bastions of the City, making them, with their country estates and hereditary peerages, more English than the originals.

This whole cosy world was abruptly shattered in the 1980s. The Americans, while active in bonds, had previously ignored British equities in favour of their own stock markets. But by the end of the 1970s they came to realise that modern communications would allow them to track any market in the world. They therefore grew much more international in outlook and came pouring off the planes as if in preparation for some latter-day D-Day, to attack the traditional customer base of the City. The invasion was unprecedented in its size and scale.

There was an additional reason for concern. In 1979 the new Conservative British Government lifted exchange controls and sparked off a massive surge in overseas investment by British fund managers. The Bank of England two years afterwards produced an unpublished study[3] of how the top 20 British institutions were arranging their foreign investments, and found to its horror that all but 5 per cent of the business was being funnelled through non-British brokers. This finding underlined just how uncompetitive in a world context this part of the City had become.

The blast of international competition following abolition of exchange controls was not the only force for change. Hand in hand with it came a revolution in telecommunications based on the computer and the microchip. The combination meant that money could flow at the press of a button out of the City and off to any corner of the world. The City no longer had a captive market, which it could expose to another City tradition – that of lofty and often arrogant disdain. To survive, London's financial community had to be able to be competitive in price, resources, speed, and skill with the other financial centres – New York, Hong Kong, and Tokyo. For the first time, after centuries as a monopoly, it had to learn to fight for its share of the business.

To its credit, the Bank of England read the signals and

used its influence on the Tory Government in Whitehall to
allow it to force the pace of change. The result was a
revolution unprecedented in scale in any other financial
centre. Between 1983 and 1986 the City tried in three years
to undo eighty years of ossifcation and studied indolence,
and put in place structures and trading practices which
would enable it to compete with the securities houses and
banks of America, Japan and continental Europe.

The chosen vehicle for change, as befits the City's Tory
traditions, was deregulation. Controls which restricted
entry to the Stock Exchange were swept away. Access to
the gilts market – the vitally important market in British
government securities which accounted for four-fifths of
the turnover on the Stock Exchange – was opened up to 27
(originally 29) fiercely competitive firms, many of them
American, in place of the cosy club formerly operated by
the Bank of England, via the Government Broker.

The revolution came, as revolutions do, with startling
suddenness, but the causes were there for all to see had
they chosen to look. As Britain's international role declined and the Empire that the City had financed withered
away, so the City's arteries began to harden – but slowly,
and imperceptibly, so that no one realised just how the
currents of international finance were beginning to pass it
by. London had always been better at banking than at
buying and selling shares. But the Third World debt crisis
stopped banking in its tracks in the early 1980s and led
companies to borrow in the share markets instead. They
found that they could borrow direct from investors more
cheaply than the banks could provide them with funds and
began to take advantage of the fact. But they found London
expensive because of the fees needed to satisfy all the
various compartments of the City.

Two far-reaching changes were proposed for the Stock
Exchange. First, the guaranteed minimum commissions
which brokers levied on every purchase or sale of shares
became a thing of the past. When that went, so too did the
guaranteed income of the nation's stockbrokers – an
income from a non-competitive system which allowed even
the smallest firm a cosy prosperity in all but the toughest

times. Secondly, the strict single-capacity system of working was broken down and in its place there sprang up the
mighty all-purpose conglomerates, combining banking,
broking and jobbing under one roof, and often with foreign
senior partners or owners.

The upheaval in Britain eventually caused reactions in
other European financial centres. Deregulation in London
forced similar moves in all the other major capital markets
on the Continent. But the authorities there failed to
respond in time to stop a major migration of European
financial institutions to London. For the first time the City
began to look towards the Continent as well as the
Anglo-Saxon world, and the Continent looked to it. The
Square Mile began to appear like the Wall Street of
Europe.

The major continental banking houses committed themselves and their capital to London in what was a significant change of emphasis. The Swiss banks, which traditionally had never moved outside their home country,
arrived in force. Union Bank of Switzerland bought up
Phillips and Drew, one of the biggest and most diverse
brokers, with a strong research team, a big gilts and
corporate finance business, and a substantial fund management side. Crédit Suisse took control of Buckmaster
and Moore, a smaller but still successful brokerage. Savory
Milln changed hands twice before settling with Swiss
Banking Corporation. Quilter Goodison linked up with the
French firm Paribas, and Deutsche Bank took a five per
cent stake in Morgan Grenfell, which it then used to
initiate a series of staff exchanges to tap Morgan's corporate finance expertise.

These European links hold out the prospect of a major
new area of business for the City. It could at last become
the natural financial centre for continental Europe.

Who made the money

In the early 1980s the difference between the successful
and unsuccessful areas of the City was an indictment of the
establishment. The areas where the City of London had done

well were areas where the establishment had been weak, and where innovative and aggressive foreign competitors, usually Americans, were allowed in. Often where the establishment was strong the performance was poor.

As shown in Table 4.2 the overseas earnings of the City, compiled from official statistics, give broad support to this judgement. The City was successful in the development of money markets, foreign-exchange trading and international banking, all of which showed through in the massive figures for banking earnings, which were £2,071 million in 1985. The UK banks participated in this, but the real engine of growth was the Eurodollar market, and the active presence in it of the London offices of at least 400 foreign banks, more than 100 of them American. In fact, in the mid-1980s there were more American banks in the

Table 4.2 Overseas earnings of UK financial institutions (£m.)

	1980	1981	1982	1983	1984	1985
Banking	160	900	988	1,556	2,315	2,071
Insurance:						
Companies	412	486	573	915	1,063	1,412
Lloyd's	341	382	475	563	564	1,208
Brokers	243	314	384	451	535	664
debits*	28	29	11	−34	−34	−34
Total Ins.	968	1,153	1,421	1,963	2,196	3,318
Export houses	160	119	234	275	326	350
Pension Funds	87	107	323	454	548	692
Commodities	180	160	215	350	342	268
Baltic Exchange	181	287	246	246	270	229
Investment Trusts	82	91	116	162	175	159
Other brokerage	89	93	109	141	174	195
Unit trusts	33	39	61	104	127	100
Stock Exchange	43	34	44	71	93	106
Leasing	14	43	68	64	72	66
Lloyd's Register of						
Shipping	23	32	37	33	29	29
Grand Total	2,020	3,138	3,862	5,419	6,667	7,583

* Direct investment income due to overseas parents of UK branches, etc.
Source: Committee on Invisible Exports and Central Statistical Office, Balance of Payments Pink Book

City than there were in New York. It was to the City's credit, however that it was the financial centre which invented the Eurodollar and had the flexibility and freedom from restriction to give the market a home – even if subsequently it lost the actual business to foreign houses.

The biggest money earner is insurance, made up of Lloyd's, the specialist insurance market, brokers like CE Heath and Sedgwick, and the companies themselves, giants like Commercial Union and General Accident. All have huge overseas businesses which are highly successful, and which continue to win business in spite of the growth of local insurance industries in the countries in which they operate. London remains the international centre for insurance.

Next comes banking, an activity which includes the profits on the £90 billion a day which London turns over in the foreign-exchange market, making it the largest centre for such activity in the world; the vastly successful Eurobond market which is the largest non-government loan market in the world; and of course conventional banking business. British banks have had the dominant share of world international lending for more than 100 years and are clinging on to the bulk of that business, in spite of the growth of the Japanese banks and the vigorous competition from the United States. Some 450 foreign banks now have offices in the City, making it unquestionably the world's international banking centre.

A third area where the City has a world lead is in international money management – the investment of cash in markets other than the domestic – which is demonstrated by the foreign earnings of pension funds, investment trusts and unit trusts. Mercury Asset Management revealed when it went public in 1987 that just under a tenth of the money it had under management – £1.6 billion out of £17.6 billion – came from overseas clients,[4] and it also showed that by the end of 1986 roughly one third of the cash was invested in overseas equities and fixed interest securities. This is a skill which is in increasing demand, and it is one which promises to become an even greater source of revenue in the future.

The areas where the City did worst were in securities trading and commodities, both in their different ways bastions of the establishment. The Stock Exchange was particularly disappointing, bringing in foreign revenue of only £106 million in 1985, which, considering it was the third largest stock exchange in the world after New York and Tokyo, was very poor. It reflected the failure of the Exchange to develop a position on the world stage by adapting its structures to the new business climate. Not only did its member firms fail to make an impact in Wall Street – though some met with success in Hong Kong and the Far East – but it failed to capture much of the international Eurodollar business on its doorstep and even more alarmingly, as we have seen, failed even to handle the funds which British investing institutions were funnelling out of London into foreign markets. In spite of its international traditions as the financier to an empire, in the post-war period it withdrew into a domestic and comfortably unambitious shell.

Change on the Exchange

The history of the Stock Exchange in the 1960s and 1970s sums up much that was wrong with establishment attitudes in the City. The need for change had been perceived but it proved impossible for the Stock Exchange Council to respond on an appropriate scale because of the threat posed to the members' vested interests in the *status quo*. Changes therefore came in piecemeal without any overall strategy, and this ultimately meant that they were insufficiently radical. Only in the early 1980s when it became apparent that the London market would become an international backwater unless it modernised did the floodgates open. And then it was because the government and the Bank of England forced the Council to change, not because it wanted to do so itself.

The revolution, known as Big Bang, came to be identified with the then Chairman of the Exchange, Sir Nicholas Goodison – on the surface an unlikely revolutionary, given his establishment background. And yet his period as a stockbroker had been one of tremendous change. When he joined the Stock Exchange in 1958 the UK economy was only just being freed from many of its post-war controls. The excess levy on company profits went in 1954, the controls on building in 1958 and the artificial distinction between distributed and undistributed profits the same year. The cult of the equity had not yet arrived and the investing public had still to realise that the income from shares could rise faster than the rate of inflation. Funded pension schemes were few and far between and institutional investors accounted for a mere 18 per cent of the equity holdings.

The rules for this market reflected the age, though they had evolved in the early days of the century. Brokers and jobbers pursued separate and distinct roles, the former as agent, the latter as principal, and because neither poached on the other all the business was funnelled into the market. It not only prospered but, perhaps because its members did so well, they were also mostly honest, and this led to a high degree of investor protection. There was also a great deal of choice, and the market supported some 313 firms of brokers and 108 firms of jobbers in London alone. They were nearly all partnerships, and as the then tax law restricted them to no more than 20 partners, they remained quite small, with no single group of firms dominant. The market's foreign involvement consisted of a large market in gold stocks, dollar stocks and other overseas securities derived from Britain's overseas traditions.

The next decade saw a transformation. Institutional investors grew in number and importance – as did the number of analysts – till they accounted for some three-quarters of the total holdings of equities. High-spending governments and institutions hungry for gilt-edged stocks brought about an explosion in government funding, until by the mid-1980s these securities accounted for three-quarters of the market. This forced some change on the firms in the market. Bigger clients demanded bigger and more sophisticated firms to service them. Brokers had to develop research facilities where none had existed before,

while jobbers had to consolidate into larger units to be able
to take on to their books the massive lines of stock in which
the institutions liked to deal, and to be able at the same
time to spread their risks beyond one sector of the market.
The result was that by 1980 there were only 103 broking
firms (against 303) in London and, even more startling,
only 14 jobbing firms against 108.

Meanwhile the gold market dwindled, overseas securities declined and dollar stocks faded away, partly because
exchange controls made dealing difficult, partly because
foreign, and particularly North American, brokers came to
London and institutions found it easier to buy American
shares through them, direct from the New York market,
rather than dealing at one remove through London. By
persuading major clients of the merits of more and more
overseas shares, foreign firms began to challenge London
for commissions and business.

In this they were, of course, aided by the changes in
communications. In the late 1950s there was trunk
dialling, and clients would write or cable their instruc-
tions. Telephones in the 1980s still caused frustration, but
the technology had changed out of all recognition. It was
now as easy to get a price and size from the New York
market as it was from the floor a few hundred yards away
in London.

The more adventurous British brokers went overseas to
try to break into foreign markets. They met with some
limited success when the Stock Exchange changed its rules
in 1970 to allow them to compete on equal terms in
overseas markets by following local practice, even if what
they did there was against London's restrictive and in
many ways archaic trading rules. But a partner trying to
develop foreign business was often thought by his more
conservative peers simply to be having a good time and the
pressure was always to stay at home.[5] The handful of
exceptions like Vickers Da Costa and W I Carr were among
the few willing to commit enough capital to foreign markets to make an impact.

Meanwhile at home the Stock Exchange dug in against a
similar loosening to meet the challenge and different

trading techniques being introduced by American firms' offices in London, partly because of natural caution, partly because it feared, with justification, that any liberalisation in the trading of overseas stocks in London would inevitably spill over into the domestic securities market. It would then inevitably threaten the single-capacity system – the separation of jobber and broker – on which the guaranteed prosperity of the market was based, and bring about a degree of upheaval, competition and disruption which the practitioners on the Council were not prepared to contemplate.

The 1960s and 1970s were a period of widespread change, but always small-scale and gradual, some in response to the pressures outlined above, some in anticipation of them. But two changes are particularly noteworthy. First, in 1967 the rule restricting partnerships to 20 people was abolished, and this sparked off a gradual move to bigger and more powerful firms – a move which was given added impetus in the consolidations and mergers which followed the fringe bank crisis and Stock Exchange crash of 1974–5.

Secondly, the increasing size of firms, and their parallel need for more capital, prompted the Stock Exchange in 1969 to meet the problem by relaxing the rule on outside ownership. It permitted firms to become companies and to have outside shareholders, in a move which was highly significant, though barely appreciated at the time. From that date firms were free to sell 100 per cent of their equity to outsiders if they so wished. It was a change which could have allowed for the re-capitalising of the industry to enable it to return to the world stage it had vacated with the decline of the Empire. This did not happen, however, because typically there was still a crucial restriction to protect the structure of the market. Any one outside shareholder was confined to owning only 10 per cent of a member firm, so that the outsider could not dominate the member firm nor force it to change the nature of its Stock Exchange activities. Nor could several outside shareholders – for example, the banks – get together and force changes on the entire market by exerting pressure through their broking house investments.

The pressures on the market continued, however, and the demands for capital to meet foreign competition and expand overseas continued to grow, particularly after the incoming Tory Government abolished exchange controls in 1979. Institutional investors became ever more powerful and began to demand lower commissions on the vast amount of business they funnelled through brokers. Brokers in turn began to look at ways in which they could meet this demand, and the scale of miminum commissions on institutional business was gradually forced down.

The jobbers in their turn had been feeling the pinch brought about by the ever bigger clients. A Monopolies Commission report examined a proposed merger between two member firms, Smith Brothers and Bisgood Bishop, in 1977 in the course of which it discovered that the business in the leading stocks favoured by the institutions was not profitable.[6] It therefore became obvious that they, the jobbers, would be hard pressed to survive a bear market without further rationalisation, which would end up with one or two firms dominating the market. And that would spell the end effectively of competition between jobbers, and make the single-capacity system unworkable.

These long-term trends went largely unnoticed among most of the people making a daily living in the market, and progress was steady rather than spectacular. It was not until 1982 that the Stock Exchange went further down the path it had begun to tread thirteen years previously and raised the limit on outside shareholdings to 29.9 per cent, the point at which, according to British takeover convention, effective control passes to the shareholder. The reason 100 per cent single outside ownership remained prohibited was again logical. The Bank of England and the Government failed at that time to give the clear lead they were later to find necessary. There was no guidance on whether the banks ought to be encouraged to become major players in the securities market, while the Stock Exchange, with the Latin American debt crisis looming, had good reason to be concerned that any decision to admit them would irrevocably change the financial system. The Council was naturally reluctant to take such a fundamental decision casually, particularly as it was not convinced that the single-capacity system should be swept away – as it was bound to be if major new players flooded the market with capital.

In practice therefore the evolution was too slow. The Stock Exchange Council in general and the bulk of its membership were conservative, and a comfortable prosperity limited their horizons. While US firms added new services and pushed into overseas markets, the British securities industry changed little. As a result, by the 1980s British firms were tiny compared to the American giants – the largest British firms like Cazenove, Scrimgeour or Capel employing 400 compared to 40,000 for Merrill Lynch, the giant American house, or 3,700 for Bear Stearns, a firm which is only in seventh place in the American listings.

This reluctance to change simply meant that the pressure built up till it became irrestistible, but by then it was too late to adapt the conventional broking and jobbing system to cope with the new situation. The changes needed were so large-scale and so fundamental for both – involving a massive injection of capital, complete re-equipment with advanced technology systems, and the learning of so many new skills – that they were beyond the means of either broker of jobber independently. So the majority of them sold out, and independent British stockbroking and jobbing, which had been a basic plank of the City, all but vanished in the space of two years between 1984 and 1986. They were bought by the banks, the firms with the capital who were prepared to pay to get access to the securities markets. Only Cazenove, from among the old Stock Exchange, remained as the final sizeable independent representative of the old ways.

Perhaps the most instructive twist in the long saga came right at the end. When the Stock Exchange Council realised that the independent life of the securities firms was coming to an end, it pushed through one last change of rules. Commissions were increased with effect from 1982. This meant that for the last few months of their lives, the

income of the broking community was substantially
increased, and this allowed them to command much higher
prices than anyone had anticipated when they came to sell
out. For example, Kleinwort Benson paid £40 million for
Grieveson Grant, and Barclays £80 million for Wedd
Durlacher and £40 million for De Zoete and Bevan. Cynics
termed them the largest redundancy payments in history.

Change for the discount houses

Change for the discount houses was every bit as traumatic
as it was for the Stock Exchange member firms. For more
than 100 years discount houses had operated in a small
pool in the shadow of the Bank of England, as part of the
inner core of the City establishment. Their primary role
was to act as intermediaries between the Bank and the big
clearing banks in the Treasury Bill market – the extreme
short end of the government funding programme.

As we saw in Chapter 3, when the Bank of England
decided that the market for government debt had to be
modernised and enlarged if it was to cope with the demand
for funds required by Whitehall, the discount houses found
themselves in a different world. In 1986 the Bank recast
the gilt-edged market along American lines, with 27 (originally 29) primary dealers taking over the roles of brokers
and jobbers, and the Government Broker's role being taken
over by the Bank itself. And the shock waves from these
fundamental changes in turn forced changes in the nine-
strong discount market.

How the houses met this challenge depended partly on
their size, partly on their philosophy. Unlike the Stock
Exchange firms, the bigger discount houses were in a
stronger position in making the switch than was generally
realised. First, they were much larger than the outside
world had thought and had the capital – at least initially –
to act as market-makers in the new gilts regime. The
largest, Gerrard and National, was estimated to have
capital of around £100 million.

They also had the skills, and saw themselves as among
the most experienced market-makers in the City – more so

than most Stock Exchange firms. This was because the role
of the discount house had already changed after the
traumas of the fringe bank crisis in 1974–5. Several of
them realised then that future prosperity could only be
assured if they were prepared to make markets in Treasury Bills in both fair weather and foul. As a result, those
who opted for market making – and they include the three
largest houses – built up a reservoir of what emerged as
one of the scarcest skills in the City. By 1986 they had had
more than ten years of experience taking positions, living
with risk, and using the futures markets to hedge their
book.

Nevertheless, though the leading firms have proved
adaptable, the market as a whole has died as a specialist
industry and taken with it more than half of its practitioners. The old cosy club has gone, and all the smaller firms
have been forced to seek refuge under the wing of larger
securities houses, where they will be just another department. It was not the firms' fault perhaps. The City had
created a market and a type of organisation which was
unique but which could not be adapted to the changing
world. Those independent discount houses which survive
are discount houses in name, but the range of business
they do now has changed beyond recognition.

The challenge of financial futures

The major innovation in world financial markets in the
1970s was the development of financial futures. They rose
out of the currency and interest-rate upheavals of that
decade and provided a way for companies and institutions
to hedge (or insure) against such fluctuations. They were
proof of the ingenuity of market men and their ability to
come up with new products to meet changing needs. These
dynamic new markets were not, however, the product of
financial minds in London. Rather they were the creation
of bored market men in Chicago, men whose previous experience of futures trading had been in grain and pork
bellies. They were also a ready answer to the needs of the
American securities industry, where firms which combined

market making and distribution, in the way London was to follow eleven years later, needed futures markets to lay off the risks they were running. Once they realised the potential of financial futures, they developed sophisticated risk management strategies by taking positions in the conventional equity and bond market and laying off the risk in the financial futures markets. And this led to a massive increase in the turnover of those markets.

There were other reasons why such developments did not happen in Britain. The structure of British markets made innovation less likely than in the United States.[7] American markets were innovative because market men there traded as individuals on their own account; they were therefore continually on the lookout for new contracts to trade, to boost their income. In London, however, membership of the commodity markets where futures trading was developed, was in the hands of old established companies, and most traders were employees rather than acting on their own account. The innovative individual was thus stifled by the bureaucracy, not just within his own firm, but beyond that in the Councils of members which ran the markets.

The Baltic Exchange in London, perhaps the most stately market in the world, faced a similar challenge. Between pillars of Parian marble, in light filtered through a stained glass window, the Baltic's members gathered each morning, even in the 1980s, to broke the world's shipping cargoes as they had done in this building since the turn of the century. But the glorious past did not pay the rent, and the Baltic sought to compensate for the decline in shipping by building up a futures business. The attack was two-pronged. First, to link the shipping expertise with the new techniques of financial futures in order to trade a freight futures index – a device which would allow shippers to lock in forward freight rates by buying or selling the index. Second, to develop as the EEC agricultural futures market by developing futures contracts in pigmeat, beef, potatoes, grain and various other commodities.

These initiatives were painfully slow to develop, however, because top people in the City have never seen the need for marketing, regarding it as distasteful, brash, 'American', and possibly even damaging to what they consider the City's most valuable asset, its good name. New ventures were invariably launched on a shoestring. These new markets had a tiny capital which was barely enough to see them through a couple of years of lean trading, let alone to take the marketing message to the world. Again this was partly because all the initiatives had their origins in small cottage industries, but it contrasted bleakly with the fanfare which accompanied every American initiative.

A limited recognition of the realities of the 1980s came when the newly created outside agency, the Securities and Investments Board, forced the Exchanges to produce rule books and other procedures designed for investor protection, in 1987. Under pressure to cut regulatory costs and conform to the requirements of SIB, the London Potato Futures Association, the London Meat Futures Association and the Soya Bean Meal Futures Association decided to amalgamate into a new Agricultural Futures Exchange. But two, the grain market and the freight market, refused to come in at the beginning. Worse, the creation of the agricultural market was also in part a snub for the much larger London Commodity Exchange, which at the suggestion of the Bank of England, had contacted all the Baltic markets suggesting that they merged with the LCE.[8] A similar approach had been made to the London Metal Exchange, when it was reeling from the default of governments underwriting the International Tin Agreement and the subsequent law suit. But it too was rebuffed.

Most worrying for the future of the City, these divisions and disappointments, when set alongside the American single-mindedness and success, suggested that good ideas alone were not enough. They needed money, energy and commitment to make them viable in a world context. All too often the combination was not forthcoming in the City. While the Baltic struggled to persuade people to trade freight futures in the Square Mile, rival American exchanges formed reciprocal trading agreements with new markets in Singapore and Sydney which allowed contracts bought in one market to be sold without problems in another on the other side of the world. Against such barn-storming the City's initiatives were puny.

Internal rivalries

The petty-mindedness of the Baltic markets was not an isolated occurrence. The City was slow to meet the challenge from abroad because the new markets which arose out of the volatile economic conditions of the 1970s cut across traditional demarcation lines. This meant that the City's specialist firms could not respond without treading on the turf of other firms. When they did stray into other areas it usually meant trouble.

This was vividly illustrated by the commodity market's proposal to set up a gold futures market in the early 1980s. The move was at first resisted by the big five gold bullion dealers, Sharps Pixley, Rothschild, Mocatta and Goldsmid, Johnson Matthey and Samuel Montagu, who feared it might damage their business and who considered themselves much better qualified to deal in gold than were members of the futures markets. Realising that head-on opposition would lay them open to accusations of self-interest, the members of the ring instead undermined the market indirectly. They used their influence with the Bank of England to have the new contract designated in sterling, ostensibly because this would not cause confusion with their twice-daily price fixings of the bullion price in dollars. But gold was priced in dollars across the world, and the use of another currency meant that it would never be taken seriously. As a result, the market never established itself. The chance to generate extra business for the City was lost and the market closed down in 1985.

Similar rivalries surfaced in the long negotiations to set up the London International Financial Futures Exchange, which was finally opened seven years after similar markets opened in Chicago. When Liffe was being formed the establishment and the newcomers were again at odds.[9] Throughout the period when its feasibility was being assessed much of the City were of the opinion that the Bank of England would never agree to its being set up. Its eventual creation in 1982 was a watershed. It came to symbolise the breaking down of barriers and the end of the single-capacity tradition and provided valuable experience for the more imaginative stockbroking firms like Phillips and Drew, who seized the opportunity to diversify away from their traditional stock market business.

Its membership reflected the changing pattern of the age. Clearing banks linked up with commodity dealers. British and American firms traded side by side. Establishment pillars like Gerrard and National formed joint ventures and pooled expertise with the successful commodity dealer, Intercommodities. Of the 373 membership seats in Liffe when it opened, UK commodity brokers held 87, members of the Stock Exchange 42, UK investment brokers 23, UK banks 56, overseas banks 74, overseas investment brokers 39, and overseas commodity brokers 52. From the beginning Liffe was quite independent of all previous markets, and because of this its membership was broadly based rather than specialist. It was very much a forerunner of the way other markets would also have to change. For those who cared to notice – and few did – Liffe was a clear demonstration that fundamental changes were taking place and that the City would never be the same again.

But there were hiccoughs. In 1985 Liffe and the Stock Exchange both wanted to expand into the new area of traded options in currencies. Traded options were part of the Stock Exchange turf; currency hedges were within Liffe's orbit. Both markets saw the chance of substantial profits in the future if they could establish a successful contract; neither would back down, and both launched almost identical contracts in currency-traded options. In terms of the business at stake the dispute was not significant to either market, and the competition could hardly be described as ferocious. But it was a niggling reminder of the City's ability to shoot itself in the foot. It had few enough resources – both human and material – to meet the American challenge, and it did little to assist its survival as a major world centre by squandering them on internecine disputes.

The new market in government securities

The Eurodollar market was the first and Liffe was the second of the markets to illustrate how the names of the players in the City were changing. But the message was still not apparent because these markets were new. It was only when change came to one of the most basic of the City institutions that it became obvious to all. This was the case in the market for government debt, known in London as gilts.

The new gilts market provided an instant guide to the emerging power structure in the City and the firms which had the grit and determination to survive. It showed how the traditional merchant banks had dropped out and how the City had become international. Table 4.3 lists the founding 29 primary dealers in alphabetical order, though two, Bank of America and Union Discount, withdrew before the market opened because they considered the climate too competitive, and Lloyds withdrew later.

The remarkable thing about this list is the names which are not there. Rothschilds did not have the resources or the stomach to move into the market, and neither did Schroders, Hambros or Robert Fleming. Indeed, of the inner circle of 16 Accepting Houses only six were represented – Barings, Warburg through Rowe and Pitman, Kleinwort Benson, Montagu, Morgan Grenfell and Hill Samuel. The rest of the great names have to be considered to have fallen by the wayside, or at least no longer to regard themselves as world players.

Remarkable too are the names which are in the securities business for the first time. All four clearing banks, Barclays, Lloyds (briefly), Midland (Montagu) and National Westminster (County), are there, underlining the new commitment of these organisations to the hitherto closed world of securities trading. Three of the nine discount houses, Gerrard and National, Alexanders and Cater Allen, have made the move – Union Discount having pulled out – also showing how this part of the City was alert enough to change.

Four American organisations, B.T. Gilts, Salomon, Gold-

Table 4.3 Primary dealers in the gilt-edged market

Firm	Parent Nationality
Aitken Campbell	British
Akroyd Rowe & Pitman Mullens	British
Alexanders, Laing and Cruikshank	British
Bank of America	American
Barclays de Zoete Wedd	British
Baring, Wilson & Watford	British
B.T. Gilts	American
Cater Allen Holdings	British
Chase, Laurie and Simon	American
Citicorp Scrimgeour Vickers	American
County Holdings	British
CSFB (Gilts)	Swiss/American
Gerrard & National	British
Goldman Sachs Government Securities UK	American
Greenwell Montagu Gilt-Edged	British
Hill Samuel Wood Mackenzie Sterling Debt	British*
Hoare Govett Sterling Bonds	American
James Capel Gilts	Hong Kong
Kleinwort Grieveson Charlesworth	British
Lloyds Bank Group	British
Merrill Lynch Giles & Creswell	American
Messel/Shearson Lehman	American
Morgan Grenfell Government Securities	British
Morgan Guaranty Gilts	American
Orion Royal Bank/Kitcat & Aitken	Canadian
Phillips and Drew Moulsdale	Swiss
Prudential Bache/Clive Discount	American
Salomon Brothers UK	American
Union Discount Securities	British

man Sachs and Bank of America were members in their own right without any local tie-up, underlining the confidence and aggressiveness of their competition. Others, both American and European, operated through their newly purchased formerly British stockbroking arms.

The market has changed and the City has survived despite the faltering initiatives and missed opportunities out-

* At the time of writing, about to be taken over by Union Bank of Switzerland.

lined in this chapter. The services the City provides are still in demand. But whether the firms which provide these services can remain in British hands or will be swamped by foreign competition is something to be considered in a later chapter.

5

How Honest is the City?

Critics of the City say that it is layered with dishonesty, and by and large the critics are right. Throughout the City, in the Stock Exchange, in Lloyd's and in the Eurobond markets, those on the inside conspire, whether consciously or unconsciously, to exploit their position to the disadvantage of those on the outside. But it is rarely a dishonesty which takes the form of outright fraud – though there are cases of that. Rather it is a dishonesty which allows those on the inside of the financial markets to provide a service to the users of the markets which is usually good, but rarely quite as good as it ought to be. And the difference is the excess profit creamed off in various ways by City institutions, a profit of which the clients are unaware but which means that, as well as earning their bread and butter, in the City they also earn a little pot of honey.

The cure for this institutionalised deception is competition coupled with full disclosure: ferocious price-cutting competition on the American model which would ensure that the client got the best deal, and the public availability of full information so that clients could make informed choices. In the late 1970s such competition began to appear, and the opportunities to take advantage of the client, without the client's knowledge, correspondingly decreased.

But this relative improvement in behaviour was largely confined to the most public of markets, the Stock Exchange and the trading of Eurobonds. In other more specialised areas of activity old habits were harder to shift. Even in 1986, for example, the Sterling Deposit Brokers Association secretly forced several of its 20 member firms to disgorge hundreds of thousands of pounds of excess profits, after the independent local authority watchdog, the Audit Commission, discovered they had been made at the expense of local authority clients. The brokers were charging the authorities inflated prices for stock they bought on their behalf, taking advantage of the fact that the section of the money markets where local authorities borrowed money and invested surplus funds has no clear price reporting system, and it is therefore difficult for clients to judge whether the prices they are quoted are honest. The Bank of England has the responsibility for policing the wholesale money markets, but no brokers were struck off the Bank's list of 'fit and proper' accredited brokers as a result of the scandal, nor were they ever named in public.[1]

The recurring dishonesty of the City is therefore, at least in part, a consequence of its secretive culture and its structural organisation with its dependence on close-knit non-competitive groups of insiders. Only if the structure is changed fundamentally, will the dishonesty be eliminated.

Conflicts of interest

Ironically, the major change of structure to have taken place in the 1980s – the reorganisation of the Stock Exchange into huge international conglomerates – brought with it a rash of new problems, to replace those which it has partly solved. The single-capacity system had been designed, at least in theory, to prevent the more blatant demonstrations of conflict of interest between financial agent and client. But post-Big Bang the danger of such conflicts of interest, and their damage to both the client and the good name of the market, loomed very large indeed.

The main technique for controlling the abuses inherent

in these conflicts of interest and the unfair use of inside information depends totally on the honesty and integrity of those working in the markets. It is the system known as Chinese Walls.

Shortly after he was elected in the early 1930s, and immediately following a particularly trying foreign policy reverse, the American President Franklin D. Roosevelt uttered a phrase which made barely an impact at the time, and which was consigned to be forgotten for almost 50 years. In the late 1980s, however, it was the phrase on the lips of everyone in the City. It arouses cynicism in some, disbelief in others and high emotions in all. FDR, in his original phrase, spoke of the Chinese wall of silence. The City, in its shorthand way, takes the silence as read, and refers to Chinese walls as a system for maintaining secrecy between departments in its institutions.

Chinese walls is a silly term for a vitally important principle – namely, that when a professional person in a securities house or similar organisation learns facts or plans which it would be profitable for people in other departments of the organisation to know, he keeps his mouth firmly shut. Thus, for example, if the corporate finance department of a merchant bank is planning with a client to launch a takeover bid, then it would not tell the fund managers in another department of the bank. The Chinese wall is there to prevent them piling into the shares of the target company to make a quick profit, either for themselves or for the funds they manage. Alternatively, if a company briefs a research analyst from a stockbroking house that its prospects are far brighter than either the stock market or the company's competitors realise, the analyst should not trot down the corridor to the corporate finance department and arrange a takeover bid from one of those competitors.

In short, the Chinese walls concept forbids analysts, fund managers, and corporate finance people from doing what used to be normal practice in merchant banks. Even in the 1970s it was commonplace for a merchant bank to sell its investment management expertise on the back of the reputation for takeover activity of its corporate finance

department. The claim was that the investment management team would be on the inside track of all the deals,
and its portfolios would therefore outperform competitors
who did not have such information. In those days, such
claims were deemed to be perfectly respectable, though it
must be said that the more limited scope for conflicts of
interest in the single-capacity era made them substantially less of a problem than they became after Big Bang.

The potential structural problems of the new conglomerate system are so widespread that it is hard to see how it
will work over a sustained period of time. In the new
houses it is accepted practice for the analyst, the salesman,
and the market-maker to operate not only under one roof
but as part of an integrated team. But the market-makers
will call the tune because, as commissions decline, they are
the ones to make the money, and this calling of the tune
will immediately put the Chinese walls under pressure. To
take an obvious example, who has first sight of a recommendation prepared by the analyst which is likely to cause
a spurt in the price of a share? Is it the clients of the firm,
or is it the in-house market-maker?

Those who say that the market-maker should see the
analyst's recommendations first are advocates of what is
called front-running. They argue that it is necessary for
the market-maker to have a block of stock on his books in
order to satisfy in an orderly way the demand generated by
the recommendation. It would do no one any good, they
say, if the client who wanted to buy was told that there was
no stock available at the price mentioned in the analyst's
recommendation. Indeed, the waste of time involved might
well irritate the client to such an extent that he would take
his business elsewhere. There will be no shortage of rival
investment houses encouraging him to do just that. The
counter-argument against front-running is that, if the
market-maker buys first, then he is buying in front of the
news. He therefore has an advantage over the client, and
stands to profit disproportionately at the client's expense.

It is hard to take a rigid line on front-running. It is an
issue which has divided the City and led to some analysts
moving on in search of houses which do not practise it,

while others find it causes them no qualms. But the dilemma is still greater if one probes a little deeper. Is it not possible that when markets get very difficult and the profitability or even the viability of the securities house is threatened, the analyst might be pressured to recommend a share specifically to yield a profit to the market-maker and help the house over its difficulties?

Pressure can be exerted in other ways, as, for example, when the chief executive of a firm looks down over the walls from on high, and acts on the basis of the knowledge he gleans to further the interest of the firm as a whole. This happened when Hill Samuel's corporate finance department was defending AE, a motor component company, against a takeover in 1986. Hill Samuel's investment management department, which was banned from talking to corporate finance, was nevertheless given an indemnity by the parent company of the bank, at the instigation of the chief executive, to compensate it for the drop in the price of the AE shares which was seen to be inevitable if the bid were to fail. This indemnity was to persuade the investment managers not to accept the bid on behalf of the funds they managed and to keep them loyal to the defence. It also helped preserve good relations with AE whose pension funds were coincidentally managed in part by Hill Samuel.

The indemnity was given by the parent company of the group and because it came from there, not from the corporate finance department, Hill Samuel's chief executive, Christopher Castleman, argued that there was no direct link between the corporate finance and the investment management departments and that the Chinese walls had not been breached.[2] Others find the argument unconvincing.

It is for such reasons, born of long experience of the City and its ways, that its major clients, the big institutional fund managers, are very sceptical about Chinese walls. They have expressed their reservations about the new system. And the richer ones have taken steps to defend themselves against it, by hiring their own teams of dealers, and by beginning to do their own research so that they do not have to rely on the adulterated product of investment

houses. It is a fitting judgement on the system that those
customers of the City who know the City best are the ones
with least faith in this aspect of self-regulation.

Insider dealing

A fundamental test of the City's honesty is its ability to
handle inside information without seeking to use it to
personal advantage, and nowhere is this problem of security and responsibility more acute than in the area of
takeover bids. Thus the movement of shares in the target
company which were bid for in the weeks before the
takeover offer became public knowledge, provides at a
glance a guide to the integrity of the City. If the City were
totally honest and leakproof there would be no untoward
movement of shares in advance of takeover bids. The more
the movement, the lower the standard of integrity.

Though dealing on inside information has been a crimin-
al offence since 1980 it is still a test which the City fails
disastrously. Table 5.1 records what happened to the
shares of all the British quoted companies which were bid
for in the spring of 1985. It shows that the vast majority of
takeover bids were leaked, which means that there was
almost continuous insider trading in the takeover arena.
The actual price of the bid was noted, and compared with
the closing price of the shares recorded on the Stock Exchange the day before the bid announcement. These two
figures were then compared with the price of the shares
four weeks previously.

Column 3 of the table shows the percentage increase in
the share price in the four weeks up to the day before the
bid was announced, and column 4 the profit to be made by
an insider dealer buying four weeks before the offer and
selling at the bid price. In 28 out of the 33 bids launched in
the first three months of 1985 the share price rose in the
four weeks before the offer. Though in nine cases the increase in the immediate pre-bid period was under 10 per
cent, in most cases the rise was substantially more. It was
also substantially in excess of any general movement in
the market, so these share price flurries cannot be blamed

Table 5.1 Share price movements before takeover bids

Target	Bidder	4-week rise	Profit
January 1985			
Butterfield Harvey	Technology Inc	+ 43%	+ 56%
Dunlop	BTR	+ 24%	− 8%
Wm Leech	C H Beazer	+ 6%	+ 37%
London & Manchester	Amalgamated Estates	+ 22%	nil
Sterling Guarantee	P & O	+ 19%	+ 22%
Trident TV	Pleasurama	+ 18%	+ 35%
February 1985			
Banro Industries	C H Industrials	+ 22%	+ 32%
Bonusbond Holdings	Promotions House	− 21%	+ 13%
Booker McConnell	Dee Corporation	+ 7%	+ 2%
Charles Hurst	Garvagh Securities	+ 11%	+ 48%
East of Scot Onshore	IFICO	+ 5%	+ 29%
Foster Brothers	Ward White	+ 33%	+ 82%
Haden	Trafalgar House	+ 17%	+ 21%
Initial	BET	+ 2%	+ 4%
Lake & Elliot	Suter	+ 14%	+ 38%
Manor National	C D Bramall	nil	+ 15%
Pauls	Harrisons & Crosfield	+ 19%	+ 57%
Petrolex	Clyde Petroleum	− 14%	nil
Pratt Engineering	600 Group	− 6%	+ 50%
Seccombe Marshal	Citicorp	+ 16%	+ 31%
Tootal	Entrad (Australia)	+ 4%	+ 8%
Unibond	Beecham	+ 13%	+ 64%
March			
Foster Brothers	Sears	+ 22%	+ 19%*
Immediate Bus Systems	Wheelabrator Int	+ 11%	nil
Ingall Industries	Gtr Midlands Coop	+ 6%	+ 16%
J & H B Jackson	Williams Holdings	+ 34%	+ 89%
Matthew Brown	Scottish & Newcastle	+ 17%	+ 57%
R P Martin	Quadrex	+ 22%	+ 30%
Routledge & Kegan Paul	Associated Book Pubs	+ 3%	+ 51%
Thames Inv & Secs	Weber Holdings	n/a	n/a
The Times Veneer Co	Corp Development Int	+ 25%	− 44%
UBM	Norcros	+ 31%	+ 34%
Waring & Gillow	Hopecastle	+ 26%	+ 37%

on a movement in share prices as a whole.

The biggest rise was the 43 per cent leap in the price of Butterfield Harvey, but it was not alone. The Foster Brothers and the Jackson shares both rose by more than 30 per cent prior to the announcement of terms, and in total more than a dozen of the bids showed pre-bid rises of over 20 per cent.

The Stock Exchange now monitors unusual price movements in shares and if, as frequently happens, the shares of a company move up sharply in front of a takeover bid, or better than expected profits, it holds an enquiry to try to find out who bought the shares and whether they were just lucky or they were acting on privileged information. Most of these enquiries come to nothing because, though it can discipline the broker, the Exchange has no power to go to the client.

However, in some 93 cases in the first six years of operation of the law it came to the conclusion that there was a case to answer and sent the papers to the Department of Trade and Industry to be passed on the Department of Public Prosecutions. These resulted in five cases being brought and three convictions. All the offences were very low-level, against clerks, and secretaries.[3]

These low-level prosecutions contrast sharply with the belief among senior regulators that insider dealing has been organised on an international scale and at a high level. The arrest of Geoffrey Collier, head of securities at Morgan Greenfell, allegedly for dealing in shares of AE and Cadbury Schweppes, on the basis of inside information, through a Cayman Islands company and a Los Angeles stockbroker, lent substance to this view, as did the later charge against Nahum Vaskevich, the head of corporate finance at the London headquarters of Merrill Lynch Europe. In the latter case, the American SEC alleged in a Manhattan court that he made $4.5 million[4] by dealing in or passing on information on 20 American takeover deals on which Merrill Lynch was advising. And the High Court in London was told by Department of Trade Inspectors investigating links between British civil servants and insider dealers that a civil servant and one ring had made profits of at least £10 million. The unnamed civil servant allegedly passed on confidential information about government decisions on monopoly and merger policy which was likely to move share prices once it was made public.[5]

They are thought not to be alone. Michael Feltham, head of the Stock Exchange surveillance department, admitted that the authorities could track the deals done in Britain but that 'the big fish go offshore'.[6] Of 284 inquiries in the period up to 1985 about 50 had been frustratated by the use of offshore companies, particularly those in the Carribean and in Liberia. Feltham and his colleagues believe that organised groups stand behind these offshore deals. Their members work for a variety of City institutions which receive prior information about bids, such as merchant banks, solicitors, accountancy firms and investment managers. They pass information to each other to make any suspected links with share purchases difficult to trace.

The Stock Exchange authorities are of the opinion that the burden of proof needed to make a case succeed in court is so great that the rules against insider trading are now less effectively enforced than when the Stock Exchange tried to punish offenders under its internal codes of discipline. The cynical conclusion of most observers is that unless they are very stupid, very junior, or betrayed by accomplices, as happened in the 1986–7 insider dealing scandal on Wall Street, then they are unlikely to be caught.

Manipulation of share prices

The manipulation of share prices on the Stock Exchange is big business, but while it may appear dishonest when carried out by an individual, the same thing executed by a business, a corporation, or a merchant bank may be legitimate business practice. The simplest and most common action which can in some circumstances be called dishonest is the share ramp, the pushing up of a share price so that it can be sold at a profit.

The temptation to do this is strong, because the individual investor has good reason to want to sell fast. First, his judgement may well be wrong and his reason for buying the shares could turn out to be such a non-event that it leaves the share price unmoved. This happens time and time again. Second, though his reason for buying the shares was a good one, there may turn out to be an even better one which he does not know about for selling. Perhaps the chairman is about to be arrested for fraud, perhaps a far-away competitor is about to launch a revolutionary new product which is going to wipe the company out, perhaps a government minister makes a keynote speech admitting that the entire economy is in dire straits. Whatever the reason, until the profit is in the bag, life for the investor is uncertain.

It therefore makes good commercial sense to minimise the uncertainty by trying to make things happen quickly, and the City's time-honoured way of doing this is by rumours. Spreading rumours is an industry in its own right. Everybody in the City does it, though most do it badly. Those who do it best have a following of their own. Once it becomes known that they are buying a share, others rush in after them, without even waiting to hear the rumour, on the basis that by the time they have found out all the details, it will be too late.

There are several ways to spread the word. Financial journalists are bombarded with telephone calls, often but not always anonymous, urging them to look at such and such a share and outlining the case for it. Or a broker can be sent in deliberately to buy clumsily and provoke a flurry in the share price, and this immediately attracts attention and creates a fertile climate for the subsequent rumours. Or the buyers can just keep buying remorselessly without saying why, and allow others to invent reasons for them. And most common of all are the tall stories told over a lunchtime glass of wine to the ears of gullible financial journalists and fellow brokers and investment managers. It is not unusual for a financial journalist or an investment manager to hear from a good source that a share in a small company, currently standing at 10p, will start moving up a week next Thursday, will rise to 20p over the following week, will hit a plateau and will then fall back to its starting price. Or he may be told that a share currently at 400p has assets worth 1600p and is for the first time going to announce a record profit and pay out half its assets in cash. That kind of formula is good for a swift 30 per cent rise on any share price. Or, of course, there is the favourite when people can think of no other way to get a share price moving, which is to suggest that it will shortly receive a takeover bid at substantially more than its current price.

Who is ultimately behind the manipulation rarely comes to light, as most sources will claim to have heard it from someone else and would never admit to being the principal. But equally most people are very reluctant to take a tip from someone they do not know. So who tells you becomes as important as what the story is. Needless to say, no one has ever been publicly disciplined by the Stock Exchange for spreading false rumours.

The discussion so far concerns individual attempts to manipulate a share price. This goes on, it cannot be stamped out, but in most cases it is not particularly successful. Far more fundamental to the system is the fact that a major part of the City's Stock Exchange activity is geared to just this kind of manipulation, which one could cynically describe as official share ramps.

The effort made by companies to get their share price up – to protect themselves against a takeover, to make it easier to take over someone else, to make it cheaper to raise new money by selling more shares to the existing shareholders, or simply to indulge the vanity of the chairman – is vast. Merchant banks, stockbrokers and public relations firms are the main agents who mastermind the manipulation and they are paid tens of thousands of pounds for their efforts. It goes on all the time, and the only reason it is not more visible is that the share price movements take place over a period of months or in some cases years, rather than a matter of weeks, which is the shorter time span in which the private individual manipulator is forced to operate.

The Guinness board's efforts to have their share price supported during the bid for Distillers gave a rare public glimpse of the workings of this system. Some £25 million was paid in secret through special accounts to various parties who assisted in this exercise or in other parts of the bid, and some £250 million was mobilised to support the price. Some, like the businessman Gerald Ronson, received £5 million for being heavy buyers of Guinness shares; and Ronson's stockbroker Tony Parnes of Alexanders Laing and Cruikshank, one of the most respectable firms in the City, received more than £1 million for arranging this and other support. Merchant banks, like Henry Ansbacher, chipped in as a favour to a friend; Ansbacher's chief executive Lord Spens had a close relationship with Roger Seelig of Morgan Grenfell, Guinness's advisers.

Though Guinness's share ramping was excessive, and the manipulation got out of hand, it was successfully concealed from the Stock Exchange authorities and the Takeover Panel. It was only when Ivan Boesky, the American insider dealer involved in the scheme, confessed to the US authorities who passed the information on to the British Government, that the matter came to light. It remains the City's widely held view that most major bids involve attempts to manipulate share prices and that the Guinness scandal erupted because of the extremes to which the company and its advisers went, rather than of the principle itself.

Obviously if a banker or public relations man is given the brief to raise a client's share price by 50 per cent within two years, the temptation to buy a few shares himself at the beginning of the exercise is strong, particularly because the agent can claim that he is not acting on inside information or using it to bring about the share price rise. Instead, the price is deemed to rise because the City understands the company better, has a greater appreciation of its management, and a more optimistic view of its future – all good reasons created by the publicity machine to reinforce the efforts on the brokers' part to sell the shares to the fund managers.

The widespread dissemination of favourable articles about a company is part and parcel of the effort to get its share price up. As indeed is the generous entertainment of financial journalists at everything from a box at the Miss

World Contest to two weeks in Barbados on a 'fact-finding' trip. Given the competition between newspapers and the City's seemingly insatiable appetite for the best 'gossip' about companies in the financial columns, it is perhaps inevitable that many commentators are biased in their coverage of particular companies. But this sort of publicity is only a small part of the system. Far more fundamental are the stockbrokers, for they make their living by buying and selling shares, and the key to persuading someone to buy is to give them a good story – or to issue a stockbroker's circular in which the good and bad points of the company are spelled out, and the prospects for the shares are analysed.

If a stockbroker writes an enthusiastic circular encouraging people to buy the shares after having talked to a company's management and analysed its accounts, he is doing his bit to improve market information and ultimately the allocation of resources to the most efficient companies. That is obviously a necessary part of the system. But that same broker will keep the information dark until his favoured clients have been given a private briefing and have had ample time to buy the shares they want. Only then is it released to the outside world. Thus in principle the big broker adopts the same technique as the manipulator.

Brokers make a living by persuading people to buy or sell shares, plus some fee-based income for providing other services. And sometimes their enthusiasm gets the better of them. Uncovering shares which are cheap, and encouraging people to buy them, is therefore a vast industry. Brokers are at its centre and they are therefore at the centre of a massive amount of share price manipulation.

If an individual hears a bit of company gossip on a golf course and spreads it around among his friends, then what he has done is the same in principle, though obviously on a smaller scale. But in this case he is likely in the quaint old-fashioned slang of the City to be dubbed a 'spiv'.

One of the central difficulties about passing moral judgements on the City is the fact that what is right or wrong does depend to a large degree on who is doing the deed.

Acts done by individuals may be wrong, but when carried out by large respectable houses they are part and parcel of normal business life. While that may be acceptable there is also a less defensible side to it, however. The big broker or merchant bank, a member of the City's establishment, has considerably more leeway to bend rules or to push principles to their limits, than does the newcomer firm with less of a pedigree. This is because the assumption on which self-regulation is based, particularly when those with the pedigrees are the regulators, is that established City names will do no wrong.

The individual investor and the City

> The Stock Exchange's regulatory restrictions (a word I use deliberately) have over the years enabled us to secure high standards of conduct and integrity on the part of members, member firms, employees, and to a very large extent their customers. The rules protect investors and above all maintain public confidence in the ethical and financial integrity of the stock market.

This was the position of Sir Nicholas Goodison, Chairman of the Stock Exchange, in 1985.[7] In reality the City is not always as clean as Sir Nicholas would like to believe.

Investment management

The area where the public comes most into contact with the City is in investment management. Given that in most clubs people on the inside think those on the outside to be fair game – and the City is first and foremost a club – it is not surprising that this is the area where some of the most flagrant abuses exist.

To make a considerable amount of extra money some investment managers indulge in a practice known as 'holding the name'. As an illustration, let us suppose an investment manager instructs a broker to buy 10,000 shares in ICI at 600p. If the shares rise to, say, 630p before they have to be paid for (which is several weeks later), then they are quickly sold, and the profit – £3,000 – is booked to the investment manager. If, on the other hand, the shares had fallen, they would simply have been booked to the funds under management and the loss would be borne by the clients – the unit trust holders, insurance policy holders or pension fund beneficiaries. The practice is called 'holding the name' because the name of the buyer is withheld until it is known whether the purchase is showing a profit or a loss.

A refinement of this system is the 'contract note trick'. A stockbroker who wants business from an investment manager simply bribes him by sending him the documentation on completed share deals executed without his knowledge – the contract notes – which yield fat profits to the manager. These deals are generated by the brokers buying and selling on behalf of clients for whom they have discretion. Discretionary clients pick up the bill for the trades that go sour, the profits are passed on to investment managers.

A further variation involves a stockbroker buying a substantial position in a company of modest prospects, so that he has absorbed most of the stock available in the market. By prior arrangement an investment manager then starts to buy that same stock heavily, and in the absence of available stock this forces the price substantially higher. It also creates a considerable profit on the stockbroker's holding, which is then sold to the investment manager to satisfy the buying requirements of his fund. The profit is subsequently split privately between them.

Investment management is very profitable for the City firms, though Big Bang and the reduction of commissions have cut into one of its sources of revenue – the City convention known as continuation. This concerns the profit which came from the consolidation of deals. A manager with dozens of clients whom he was taking out of ICI and putting into BTR would not sell each parcel of shares individually. Instead, he would consolidate the holdings into one large transaction which allowed him to benefit from the reduced level of commission which the Stock Exchange, even in the days of fixed commissions, applied on large parcels of business. But the individual investor was charged the full commission as if the shares had been

sold in small lots. The difference – which could be one or
two per cent of the value of the shares sold – went to the
investment manager. It is significant that the prospectus
for Mercury Asset Management when it went public a few
months after Big Bang in April 1987, warned potential
investors of the diminished profitability of the fund management business as a result of this change.[8]

Unit trust managers have a further way to boost their
income at the expense of the client through a technique
known as 'running the box'. Every unit trust quotes both a
buying and a selling price for its units, with a difference
between the two of up to five per cent of the value of the
units. If an investment manager repurchases a parcel of
units from one investor and sells them on to another, he
makes an immediate five per cent profit.

But the manager needs to persuade the new buyers to
come in. It is therefore helpful when running the box to
engineer sudden spurts in the value of the unit trusts in
order to generate buying interest. Short-term boosts can be
achieved quite legally because unit trust rules effectively
allow the managers three days grace in which to decide to
which fund they are going to allocate a share, and that is
quite sufficient to manipulate the price.

One method is for all the winners over a period to be
pumped into the fund which is meant to perform. Another
more fundamental trick is to switch the entire basis of
valuation of the fund from a bid to an offer basis – reflecting the difference between the buying and selling prices of
the underlying shares in the unit trust portfolio. This will
give a once-and-for-all boost to performance of several percentage points.

Not all the income of a fund comes from dividends on the
shares in the portfolio; short-term gains can also be
achieved by funnelling fees earned across the group into
just one trust. The main source of this extra income is from
underwriting – providing a guarantee to a merchant bank
or broker that, if called upon to do so within a period of 30
days, the manager will buy stock which one of his clients
may need to issue to complete a takeover or a rights issue.
The fee – perhaps three quarters per cent of the value of

the stock which in any event the manager is only rarely called upon to buy – is a major source of income for investment managers, and if it is all credited to one fund will make a significant impact on its performance. Short-term gains can also be achieved by allocating all the winners, bought initially in the name of the management company, to just one trust, while the duds go to a fund which is not scheduled for promotion to the public.

Investment managers do this regularly just before they ask the public to invest more money. They have discovered that the easiest way to attract new cash is to advertise a fund with a good investment performance, and they therefore go to considerable lengths to create it before launching a marketing campaign. It is possible, according to those who have practised the art, or seen others do it, to boost the performance of a fund by anything up to 20 per cent over a three month period by using these devices. Which is enough in most periods to put it to the top of the performance tables, were it not for the fact that other investment managers are doing the same thing.[9]

As investment became more complex and more volatile during the 1980s there was a trend for the investment management of pension funds to be contracted out to specialist portfolio management groups. Competition between these management groups was fierce, because it was a business of low overheads and potentially very high profits, provided sufficient contracts could be won. Different investment management groups were generally judged on their performance, by which was meant their ability to make the funds in their charge increase in value thanks to their investment policies. Those which achieved a good performance were rewarded with more funds to manage; those which were below-average performers tended to lose contracts. The independent managers therefore had a direct commercial interest in being seen to be producers of above-average performance, and this again gave rise to a series of techniques designed artificially to inflate the apparent value of the funds.

It is common practice in pension funds (which, unlike unit trusts, are allowed to hold property) to transfer com-

mercial properties sideways from an existing portfolio into
a new one at artificially low prices. The properties can then
be 're-valued' a few months later, and discovered to be
worth far more than their transfer price. This shows
through in the fund as a whole as a leap in performance.
Commercial properties, warehouses and shopping centres,
are much better for this purpose than office blocks, as
valuers frequently disagree by as much as 50 per cent
about how much a commercial property is worth, and no
one can argue that the gain is not genuine. It is not un-
known for the management company to have an extra
interest in such revaluations, in the form of a management
fee which is by agreement a percentage of the growth
recorded by the funds under management. In these circumstances it gets an added bonus of greater income as the
result of such 'performance'.

There are many other techniques which collectively enable a management company in the short term to inflate
the performance of a particular trust. But in spite of the
artificiality inherent in most claims of fund management
'performance', it is still a major feature of advertising and
the main way in which fund management groups are
judged. Individuals put their savings with investment
management groups on the basis of these performance
claims. If they knew how easy it was to manipulate the
figures they might be a lot less willing to part with their
money.

New issues

Another area where the public comes in contact with the
City, and loses, is when a company goes public – when it
sells shares on the stock market for the first time. Though
from the outside the issue may appear to be a combination
of an auction and a ballot in which all those who subscribe
seem to have an equal chance of success, this is not so,
because the two methods of new issue in common use in the
City – the placing and the offer for sale – are both widely
and openly abused to the benefit of those on the inside.

The private placing system is one of those City practices

which on the surface appears justified as benefitting the client but which in fact ensures that those on the inside get more than their fair share of successful investments. It is a simple and effective way of extending bribes and repaying favours, because it allows the broker handling the issue to deliver a parcel of shares on which there is a guaranteed profit to a named individual or fund of his choosing. The broker alone decides who gets the shares, and there is no way by which an outsider can force his way into the circle without the consent of the people handling the issue.

Placings used to be confined to companies going public for the first time, but in 1987 it became commonplace for companies to pay for small acquisitions by placing a parcel of shares with their broker, for him in turn to place or sell on to his clients. Usually such deals were accompanied by profit forecasts which boosted the share price, and of course made it easier to sell the new stock, and again put the broker in the happy position of having customers pleading to buy, and allowing him to choose who should reap the benefit.

The 1985 British Telecom share offering had a large portion of the issue allocated for placing with institutions, but large numbers of shares found their way into the pockets of individuals, when the institutions who received them in the first place, passed them on. This allowed certain individuals to receive tens of thousands of Telecom shares when the members of the public were supposed to be restricted to just 800 each.

The Stock Exchange was alerted to the fact that the allocation mechanism had been by-passed when its surveillance department picked up some unusually high share sales by individuals, and this precipitated a full-scale inquiry, details of which were subsequently leaked.[10] It emerged that National Insurance and Guarantee Corporation, a company belonging to the well-known financier and industrialist, Gerald Ronson – a man who was later to figure also in the Guinness affair – had agreed to underwrite 2 million of the shares on issue, of which it was subsequently allocated 1.1 million. Sir Philip Harris, founder of Harris Queensway the carpets retailer, sold

237,500 Telecom shares within weeks of the issue at an average profit of around 50p a share. The Stock Exchange could not establish where he had obtained his shares, but there was circumstantial evidence that they had been given or sold to him by Ronson because the authorities had established that when half of the Ronson company holding was sold through brokers Laing and Cruikshank on 10 December 1985, it instructed that the proceeds of 137,000 shares be allocated to Harris.

Anthony Solomons, the chairman of Singer and Friedlander, one of the inner circle of merchant banks, also took Telecom shares on his own account, because he believed that it was politically vital for the issue to succeed. He made a more modest £50,000 on his holding and when the matter was subsequently publicised, he gave the profits to charity.[11] And in another merchant bank the Chairman privately admitted that the directors took their institutional allocation for themselves and made six-figure sums overnight.[12]

In theory there was no reason why the other popular privatisation issues were not subject to the same possibility of abuse, except that the government laid great emphasis on trying to eliminate them. But if later privatisations were relatively clean, the pre-placings which precede many offers for sale have been and remain a major area of potential abuse.

A separate fault of the system is that, although the Stock Exchange does try to monitor the quality of all new issues to ensure that only companies of substance are sold to the public, it nevertheless tends to let its guard slip when the sponsors and directors of issues have impeccable City connections. On 1 April 1985, for instance, a company called New London Oil was sold at 135p under the sponsorship of Greenwell and Robert Fleming, a top broker and a top merchant bank. The shares enjoyed a brief flurry of popularity and then within weeks they had dropped by half. Two years later investors had lost four-fifths of their money. It was clear that the company was a disastrous investment.

There were two reasons for the problems. The first difficulty was that New London had taken over a large number of American oil prospecting partnerships in which some nine Greenwell partners had been heavy investors; they were prominent as founder shareholders of New London. These oil concessions were valued for the purpose of the issue on the basis of possible as well as proven reserves, and this method produced a valuation which was a far more optimistic basis than would have been allowed in the United States. It understandably also helped ensure that the shares proved initially popular, though, as subsequently turned out when no oil was found, for no substantial reason. Second, though the company did not have a five-year profit record, the Stock Exchange waived this requirement because the company had such a distinguished board and advisers of high standing, including of course the Greenwell partners, some of whom were on the Stock Exchange Council. The consequence was that investors had no means of judging the performance of the management, nor the soundness of its policies. New London should not have been allowed to go public when it did. It is hard not to conclude that the reason it was allowed to do so was that it was a product of the City establishment, and normal standards of inspection were not applied.[13]

Private client problems

The third way in which the individual can deal with the City is as a private client, and again, though in general he gets a good and honest service, it is common for City firms to indulge in practices which would shock most investors if they knew about them.

The simplest device is known as churning. This is the practice whereby brokers recommend to clients that they buy shares, not because they think the new investment is any better than the one being sold, but because the broker wants to generate a commission, or a profit on shares which the firm has on its books. Churning takes many forms. On one level the broker simply telephones the client when he knows he will be busy and will agree to a deal simply to put an end to the call. On a more organised scale

it occurs when clients with, say, ICI may be advised to
switch into BTR, while clients with BTR are advised to buy
ICI – an incident which came to light recently, according to
The Financial Times, when the letters justifying the
switch were inadvertently put in the wrong envelopes.
This latter kind of churning is particularly profitable, because the shares need never go near the stock market at
all. The broker simply swaps round the portfolios in his
office but the client has to pay commission or charges as if
the deal had gone through the market.

Churning is particularly prevalent in the unit trusts run
in-house by stockbrokers. A 1986 magazine survey[14]
showed that it was commonplace for the portfolio of a unit
trust run in-house to be completely turned over once every
fifteen months, and in some cases two or three times a
year. That is substantially more dealing than takes place
in the unit trust industry as a whole, where on average
portfolios turn over once every two years. And it is 10 to 15
times as much dealing as would be done if the unit trust
shares were to be traded at the same rate as shares in the
market.

In 1986 the SIB sought to ban the practice. But it was
forced to admit from the beginning that it was a hopeless
task as it was impossible to prove – though, as the SIB said,
those who are doing it know when they are doing it. The
proposal was quietly dropped.

Overrides and benefits in kind

Clients never know how much of their money is used to buy
shares, not because they are a good investment but simply
to reward a stockbroker for some perk he has steered the
fund manager's way.

The SIB proposed in its draft rules to govern conduct in
the City when the Financial Services Act came into operation, to make it illegal for brokers to give inducements to
other firms or to their staff to place business with them.[15]
Benefits in kind to be outlawed include holidays abroad
and office equipment like computers. The SIB said that
Christmas presents not exceeding £25 and modest enter-

taining would be allowed, but that 'research trips' round the Far East should be banned.

This caused something of a hollow laugh in the industry where presents of £25 are unheard of, but lavish parties at top social events and a high standard of entertaining are commonplace. Every year analysts and financial journalists embark on a round which takes in racing at Royal Ascot, the Derby, and many lesser race meetings, the Henley regatta, tennis at Wimbledon, rugby at Twickenham, the military festival at the Royal Tournament, cricket at Lords, golf at the British open, opera at Glyndebourne, polo at Cowdray Park and even the Miss World competition and ball at London's Grosvenor House Hotel. All the bills are picked up by a broker or the industrial company which is seeking to forge contacts with people in the City. The bills can be massive – probably £150 a head on food, champagne, and in summer the regulation Pimms.

It is impossible to measure the extent to which this entertaining leads to active recommendations to buy a company's shares or to fund managers diverting business to specific brokers. But the British investment manager does business with far more stockbroking firms than he needs to cover all the areas of market expertise. Five firms would be sufficient, but managers generally deal with fifteen or more, and the reason for the diversity is to respond to the favours given. The SIB recommendations to control entertaining are therefore well-intentioned, but unlikely to make much impression, given the size of the beast it is trying to slay. Henley, where one company is reputed to spend over £75,000 a year, Ascot, where a box for the day will cost over £10,000, and the others will no doubt continue to prosper.

Conclusion

The problem in any discussion of honesty in the City is that the individual City firm only cares what its peer group thinks. If Whitehall or Westminster has an occasional bout of indignation about City standards, then the City will take no notice, knowing that the storm will quickly blow over. If the attack is more direct, as when a distinguished figure like the Commissioner of the Metropolitan Police attacks the City for its failure to prevent criminals from laundering money through its financial institutions,[16] it will not be drawn into a debate with outsiders. Instead, on this occasion the Bank of England saw fit to issue a press release which ignored Sir Kenneth's central theme, but sought to belittle him on points of detail.[17]

Similarly the City cares not at all about the opinion of the public at large. For years it ignored the private investor, or placed him at the end of the queue for service, while continuing, if pressed, to take his money. It continued to do so, even when privatisation brought millions more to the City eager to become active investors. It willingly sold them shares, but gave them rough treatment when they tried to sell.

Until 1987 it was the commonly stated view of individuals in the City that, while there were a few crooks about – spivs to use their quaintly old-fashioned word – they were few and far between. They would also maintain that, while insider dealing did exist, as evidenced by the movement of share prices before bids, it certainly was not rife. The vast majority of City practitioners go about their affairs with honesty and integrity, so there is nothing for the authorities to worry about; there is nothing for them to clamp down on.

It is impossible to know how true this analysis is, but the view of SEC investigators working on insider dealing scandals in Wall Street has been that the problem is every bit as serious in London.[18] The arrests and charges laid against prominent merchant bankers in London, and the statements of regulators in the Stock Exchange, suggest that it is far more likely that dishonesty has become institutionalised. The entire ethos of the club – the way in which members help each other against the outside world – has meant that the outside world has been discriminated against. It has made it possible for the club members to protect their own interests and distort the market entirely for their own selfish ends, and for those of favoured clients. It has meant that the Stock Exchange, in spite of its posturing in pursuit of insider dealers, has, in the view of at least one prominent merchant banker,[19] been half-hearted in its commitment and incompetent in the techniques used to root the practice out. It has made it possible for fan clubs – groups of friends – to organise massive manipulation of share prices in takeover bids, which represent the most fundamental distortion of the market economy in which the City professes so strongly to believe. It has made it a way of life that in any deal where a profit was assured – which was most of them – the friends on the inside were offered their slice first before anyone on the outside was given a glimpse of it.

The criticism is not that these activities broke any of the laws of the land. But in a capitalist economy, anything which distorts the market mechanism should be viewed as dishonest. And in the City distorting the market mechanism is a way of life.

6

City and Government

The Bank of England is the City's representative in Whitehall, Westminster and the world. It is a nationalised industry, wholly owned by the taxpayer, and its officials hold rank comparable with that of equivalent officials in the Treasury.

The Bank of England's independence

As a nationalised industry it would be expected to come under the control of the government, but in common with many central banks around the world this is not in practice how it works. And as a result, though normally the relationship between the City and the Treasury is easy, there are times when it is distinctly strained.

The Treasury is, of course, much closer to the House of Commons and to political influence, and in the opinion of some people in the Bank, party politics gets in the way of its judgement. By the 1980s the power of the Bank had been considerably reduced from its former days, when it used to carry out economic policy abroad and tell the government about it only much later. Well after the First World War Britain's international economic policy was conducted not by the government of the day, whether Conservative, Labour or coalition, but by Sir Montagu Norman who was Governor of the Bank of England from 1920 to 1944. As a demonstration of his independence, Norman was wont to discuss the whole question of sterling's return to the gold standard with the US Federal Reserve Board without any effort to inform the British Government.[1]

On another occasion Norman's independent action was indirectly responsible for the fall of the government. In May 1931, Norman came to the rescue of the Austrian banking system when Credit Anstalt, the oldest and most respected Austrian bank, collapsed. The subsequent drastic budget economies, including cuts in unemployment benefit, brought the resignation of the Labour Government and Ramsay MacDonald's return to Downing Street at the head of a national government. Norman demanded further budget cuts as a condition for obtaining a supporting loan from the Americans. One of these cuts included the reduction of naval pay and sparked off what became known round the world as the Invergordon mutiny. The sight of the British navy apparently turning against its own government meant that confidence was not restored, and in September 1931 the Bank gave up the struggle and suspended the pound's link with gold.

Incidents of a similar but less dramatic nature cropped up again in the post-war world of the 1950s, though with happily less drastic consequences. This time the issue tended to be one of convertibility – whether sterling could be freely exchanged into other currencies or not. The Bank's view, reflecting the feeling of City bankers, was that sterling's role as a medium of international trade and finance would be greatly strengthened by its convertibility, and in broad terms the closer the currency to pre-war parity, the more likely it would be to have the confidence of the international community. But the British industrial sector had a different interest. Though it enjoyed a period of export-led prosperity in the immediate post-war period while its major competitors were still recovering from the wartime devastation, its medium-term interest would have been better served by an undervalued rather than an overvalued currency. The seeds were thus sown for a clash between narrow City and broad national interests.

Secret talks were held by Bank of England officials with officials of the International Monetary Fund and the US Treasury. But this time the government was better prepared. It never allowed itself to be as severely compromised as its predecessors had been in the Norman era. Senior Treasury officials discovered the Bank's intentions in time to withstand the pressure.

Any assessment of the City's impact on the country has to consider the extent to which the City pursues its own self-interest to the detriment of the country as a whole and the extent to which, as we saw in chapter 1, it appears to be a state within a state, geographically situated in Britain, but seeing itself and its destiny as somehow separate from the nation in which it is based. Specifically, does it persuade the government to adopt policies which serve the interests of the City but do longer-term damage to the country at large?

The Bank has an understandable desire to ensure the prosperity of its City constituency, and a key part of its role is to persuade governments to adopt policies which help the City. There is nothing wrong with this in principle, but it can cause difficulties. There have been two examples in recent times where this has been a major issue. The first in the early 1970s led to the fringe bank crisis and to the brink of financial collapse. The second in the 1980s led to Big Bang and deregulation of the City's financial markets – which, in the view of some in the City, could well at some time in the near future provoke a similar financial crisis.

The change of policy in 1971, which led to the fringe bank crisis of 1974, came within an ace of bringing down one of the major clearing banks and wrecking the entire British financial system. It also led to a credit squeeze and retrenchment by the banks which caused great hardship to industries and commercial activities throughout the country. Much has been made of the role of the Bank of England in its management of the crisis, of its undoubted skill and courage in launching the financial lifeboat to rescue so many sinking banks, all the while concealing the full extent of the disaster from the public so that a collapse in confidence was avoided.[2] But rather less has been said about the Bank's role in causing the crisis in the first place. Yet it was the Bank which persuaded the Heath Government[3] to adopt the policies eventually laid out in a June 1971 memorandum entitled *Competition and Credit Control*.

The incident provides a useful insight into how the Bank can influence government. In the months before the switch, the change of policy was not debated in Parliament or discussed in the newspapers. Instead it was sold to the amiable Chancellor, Anthony (now Lord) Barber – later chairman of Standard Chartered Bank – over a private dinner with key Bank of England officials in January 1971.[4] According to Douglas Jay,[5] the Treasury was mightily displeased that the Bank had dreamt up the idea and sold it to ministers without consultation. But it did nothing effective to block it. The Bank got its way.

The new policy removed the direct ceilings on the amount banks could lend, in favour of allowing the market to determine how much credit was needed through the interest-rate mechanism. 'We have in mind a system under which the allocation of credit is primarily determined by its cost', the Governor, Lord O'Brien, stated.[6] The idea seemed innocuous enough. But it led directly to a massive increase in the profitability of the banking system by allowing banks to drop their ratio of reserve assets to advances from an effective 28 per cent to just 12.5 per cent.

It also led to the most amazing credit boom the country has ever seen. Advances and deposits doubled within three years. In Jay's words 'More pounds sterling were created in these three years than in the whole of the 1200 years history of the pound since King Offa'. But the money poured not into industry, but into property and stock market speculation. Because it was based on borrowing, when the bubble burst people could not repay their debts and the entire system was threatened.

The new policy promoted by the Bank of England from the narrow perspective of the City was designed to sharpen up the City's banks and make them more profitable by making them more competitive. But it also caused an inflationary boom which led directly to industrial unrest. This in turn brought the confrontation between the Heath Government and the miners in 1972 and 1974 and the fall of the Tory Government and the return of the second Labour administration of Harold Wilson.

The parallels with the deregulation of the Stock Exchange in the 1980s are uncomfortably close. In this case the policy was initiated by Bank of England officials led by executive director David Walker, who after months of behind-the-scenes lobbying managed to persuade first Lord Cockfield and later Mr Cecil Parkinson, one a Treasury Minister and the other the Secretary of State for Trade and Industry, that London had a major role to play as the centre for international securities trading.

In July 1983 the chairman of the Stock Exchange, Sir Nicholas Goodison, was forced, under threat of a legal action against the Stock Exchange from the Office of Fair Trading, into an agreement with Parkinson to abolish fixed commissions on Stock Exchange business, in the Bank's full knowledge that this would cause the income of Stock Exchange members to plummet and spark off a massive reorganisation of the industry. The result was an unprecedented shake-up, in which outsiders, mainly commercial clearing banks from Britain and abroad, bought out brokers and recapitalised them. This brought with it the problem of insufficient business to support all the new firms. A massive increase in the amount of speculative trading as well as genuine investment demand for equities followed, which added greatly to the inherent volatility of the system, and brought with it the ever-present danger that a relatively minor setback could precipitate a re-run of the 1973 crisis, only this time with the securities houses as the casualties.

It is odd, however, how rarely the wider implications of City self-interest penetrate the political consciousness. Indeed, one of the few in-depth criticisms came from the Wilson Committee, whose report in 1980 observed:[7] 'The Bank is well regarded in financial circles both in this

country and overseas . . . (But) serious concern has also
been expressed . . . that the close relationship of the Bank
to market participants may on occasion conflict with its
obligation to provide disinterested advice to government.'

The City and monetarism

The self-interest of the City, and primarily of the Bank of
England, led also to its becoming a champion of monetarism – one of the most significant political and economic
movements of modern times – while playing little part in
its actual development.

The decade after the oil price crisis of 1973 was marked
around the world by high inflation, low economic growth
and the search for a new economic theory to replace the old
'failed' Keynesian ideas. It was the decade when monetarism became a political creed, not hedged around with the
caveats with which economists qualified its findings but a
simple slogan which was instantly appealing to politicians
and understandable to the electorate. It brought international economics down to the level of the household budget.
Countries like people had to pay their way, not live on
borrowing. Keeping tight control of the nation's purse
strings would gradually squeeze inflation out of the
system.

The conventional wisdom holds that monetarism was
ushered in by the Conservative Government of Mrs
Thatcher when it won the election in May 1979. But the
real shift from fiscal to monetary policy occurred three
years earlier in the autumn of 1976, when the then Labour
Government was forced to borrow massively from the International Monetary Fund in order to prop up confidence
in sterling and the financial markets, after a particularly
savage sterling crisis provoked by the knock-on effects of
the first oil price shock. A humiliating condition of the
loan was that IMF experts should monitor the policies and
performance of the Labour Government in meeting specific
economic targets, one of these being the control of domestic
credit expansion, which was in effect little different from
the money supply measures such as Sterling M3 which

were to be introduced later.

The view that it was the City which converted the Conservative Government to monetarism is therefore wide of the mark. Mrs Thatcher was influenced in opposition in mid-1970s by the Centre for Policy Studies, a think-tank set up by the Conservatives when they went into opposition after the 1974 electoral defeat. It produced a considerable amount of work aimed at changing the emphasis of economic thought, and examining various versions of monetarist doctrine. The City input to this was limited. The only really City-based activist in those early days was Gordon Pepper, a respected stockbroker with W. Greenwell, later Greenwell Montagu, one of the firms which did a great deal of business in the gilts market.

Indeed, with the exception of Pepper, there were few then in the City who were competent to take a view, because there were very few top-flight economists employed in the broking and banking offices. The great influx came after the IMF visit of 1976, and after the monetarist framework was in place, because it created a need for economists to analyse statistics and economic targets which were being published for the first time in Britain, and which provided the markets with yardsticks on which to measure government performance against policy, and from that performance predict the likely course of interest rates. Monetarism in fact provided the City with the financial statistics it needed to analyse the progress of government policy and the opportunity to be much more professional in its assessments of that policy.

It may not have designed the mantle of monetarism, but the City donned it with alacrity. The very simplicity of monetarist slogans which made them so appealing to politicians and electorates also made them appealing to the financial markets. The entire government economic policy could be translated into one monthly figure for the money supply (M3), which could be instantly judged as good or bad and affect the markets accordingly. It was grossly oversimplified, it was undiscerning, but the reaction of the City and financial markets to that one money supply figure came to have major repercussions for the exchange rate, interest rates and the entire financial health of the country. So much so in fact that the government, having hoisted the banner, then spent years trying to take it down again, as the Chancellor persuaded the City to be more subtle and perceptive in its analysis of economic trends.

The coming into fashion of monetarism had profound but totally unforeseen implications for the Bank of England. Until the 1970s it had been the arm of government which pursued monetary policy. It was a role, limited in scope but entirely compatible with what the Bank saw as its, and the City's, primary interest, namely, the maintenance of sound money, the continuation of sterling as an international trading currency, and thereby the preservation of the good name of the City in international finance. And it was a role which the Bank of England carried out with the skill of the Delphic oracle. It was so secretive and cryptic that no-one could ever be sure what its utterances meant or what it was doing, and it was always on hand afterwards to imply that it had engineered what did in fact turn out.

The Bank and the Conservative Government

While the City quickly learned to love monetarism, particularly after the Tories came to office, the Bank of England was less happy. During the Wilson Government, the Prime Minister's personal economic adviser, Bernard Donoughue, had organised a weekly meeting in Downing Street between the Governor of the Bank, the Chancellor of the Exchequer and the Prime Minister, as an unofficial Cabinet Committee, at which the Governor briefed the politicians on the mood of the financial markets and the implications of that mood for government policy. As a result of this ready communication, relationships between the patrician Governor Gordon Richardson and the Labour Government were generally good.[8]

The need for top policy advisers to become expert in monetarism led during the decade to a shift in the balance of power between the Treasury and the Bank of England. In the early to mid-1970s the Bank was held in awe in government circles. Under Keynesian policies the whole

112 CITY WITHIN A STATE

thrust of economic management was channelled through
fiscal policy, and this was what the Treasury concentrated
upon;[9] few understood what monetary policy was, and no
one dared to challenge the Bank's views on the subject. But
with the acceptance of monetarism by its political masters,
the Treasury realised that it would have to change. It
began to move its best people on to the monetary side, and
to get to grips with its implications.

By the time the Thatcher Government, firmly monetarist in outlook, had settled into office, the Bank was feeling
the hot breath of the Treasury's newly trained monetarists,
and advisers like the London Business School's Professor
Terry Burns, on its neck. The Treasury had by now had
three years to become much more aware of monetary policy. It strayed very firmly and deliberately on to what had
been considered the Bank's traditional area of expertise,
and inevitably it discovered that some in the Bank to
whom it had traditionally deferred were not as brilliant as
it had been led to believe.

The fault lay in the Bank's background. The Bank of
England is neither a creature of the Treasury, as the Bank
of France is of the Ministère des Finances, nor is it en-
dowed with proud autonomy like the US Federal Reserve
or the Deutsche Bundesbank. By legal statute – the 1946
Nationalisation Act – it was made formally subservient to
the Chancellor's authority. He has the right to give the
Governor directives, but though Stafford Cripps once refer-
red to the Bank as 'my creature' no Chancellor has ever
tried to exercise the right. The Bank therefore continued to
see itself as the senior partner in the Whitehall–City relationship, its independence bolstered by the fat profits it
made on its banking activities, which also allowed it to pay
salaries in line with the City merchant banks rather than
the Civil Service, and offer perks and conditions of service
unrivalled in the public sector. The Treasury, in spite of its
reputation for being the home of the brightest civil servants, paid it the compliment of an inferiority complex.

This is not a formula for easy relations. And it leads to
repeated clashes with government, no matter which party
is in power. Relations between the Bank of England and 10

Downing Street were worse in the summer of 1980 when the Conservative Government had been one year in office than they had been at any time in the 1970s under Labour. What sparked things off was the Bank's abolition of a regulation which had obliged the High Street clearing banks to freeze a proportion of their deposits, as part of the credit control policies. The resultant expansion destroyed the government's claim to have established control over the money supply, and an embarrassed Bank stood accused of either trying to undermine government policy or of being unable to implement that policy in the area where it was supposed to be expert. It was hard for the politicians to decide which was worse.

Against this background the appointment of Robin Leigh-Pemberton to succeed Governor Richardson in 1983 was a reflection of the Prime Minister's determination to have an amenable Bank in future. Mr Leigh-Pemberton was not a banker by trade, but a barrister and landowner, a former Tory chairman of Kent County Council who had graduated to the boardroom and eventually to the Chairmanship of National Westminster Bank, almost, it seemed, by chance. Hence it was suggested that his principal qualification for the job was political allegiance. This judgement is unfair to the man, but the view in the City lunch rooms in the mid-1980s was that the Prime Minister had nevertheless achieved her objective: the Bank was no longer a force in Whitehall and Westminster, and its future lay in 'looking east not west' – acting as regulator of the City and custodian of its values.

This view was strengthened by the frequent sniping of Tory politicians, and particularly Chancellor Nigel Lawson, against the Bank, when it tried to pronounce on broad economic issues. Previous Chancellors had disagreed with the Bank, but none had expressed their disagreement, and occasionally their contempt, so openly. This meant that the City, which was arguably in the mid-1980s more powerful relative to the rest of the British economy than at any time in its history because of the phenomenal growth of its international financial business in contrast to industry's pedestrian performance, was at precisely that moment distanced from the levers of power and policy-making as a result of the fall from grace of its representative, the Bank of England.

Surprisingly few in the City noticed the event or reacted in a constructive way to compensate for the power vacuum created by the Bank's problems. The newcomers, and the American banks in particular, adopted Washington-style techniques and began to lobby direct and make their own contacts. They argued, however, about specific issues, and sought specific rule changes, rather than promoting the case for the City as a whole. And the British institutions remained silent for the most part, continuing to use the old lobbying techniques of funnelling complaints through the Bank and quite failing to understand why its requests were no longer heard. As a result, the City, which in general sought little from government other than to be left alone, realised too late that it was no longer understood nor appreciated, and that while it would ignore the nation, the nation would not ignore it.

The City and the Conservative Party

While the myth of the Conservative Party and the City speaking with one voice is far from the reality, another popular belief has rather more substance to it. The City is the major single paymaster of the Conservative Party. The party is singularly unforthcoming about the size and source of its corporate contributions, and a picture can only be constructed by the laborious process of monitoring the accounts of all the largest public companies. Though many smaller companies slip through this net, it is possible to establish that the City is the major contributor in the business world to the Conservative Party and bodies associated with it. But the analysis also shows with startling clarity how small the sums actually are, and how, in contrast with political parties in the United States, the bulk of Tory party funds come from its grass roots fundraising, rather than from any form of big business.

Table 6.1 summarises the evidence. It lists political contributions in the election year of 1983, giving the total figure and the amount from that total which went to the Conservative Party. The difference between the two figures did not in the main go to other political rivals in the Labour or Alliance parties. Instead it generally went to pressure groups such as the Economic League; Aims (formerly Aims of Industry); British United Industrialists; the Centre for Policy Studies and Regional Industrial Councils. Though none of these are affiliated directly to the Conservative Party, several make donations to it, and most sponsor causes and research in tune with party thinking. So contributions made by companies in the United Kingdom generally sponsor political activity to the right of the spectrum.

The table shows that the bulk of business support for the Conservative Party comes from just four major groups: banking, insurance and finance; engineering; construction; and food, drink and tobacco. The first group, which includes the vast majority of the publicly quoted City firms, gave almost twice as much as the sector in second place, engineering. Not only was the financial sector by far the largest donor, but additional research shows that it was also the only one where the number of companies making donations increased substantially. Just at the time when the popularity of political payments was on the wane in industry, it increased in the City. The financial sector has thus become a dramatically more important source of Tory party funding in the past decade.

The two sectors of construction and finance provided 41 per cent of the total public company donations in 1983 as against only 17 per cent of the funds back in 1973. This is a truly dramatic shift of emphasis in a remarkably short time, and reflects not simply the decline of British industry over the decade, but the commensurate increase in the power of the City. The impact of its contributions is even more marked when analysed on the basis of the number of people employed. Though in employment terms the City accounts for around 10 per cent of the national workforce, roughly a third of the companies making political contributions were financial and they accounted for 28 per cent of all the money going to the party.

Table 6.1 Political contributions by sector in 1983 election year (£)

Sector	Conservatives	Total
Banking, insurance & finance	660,860	875,302
Engineering	405,190	489,642
Construction	340,735	375,735
Food, drink & tobacco	212,600	341,890
Transport	73,148	133,942
Chemicals	103,736	135,139
Building materials	76,700	86,700
Distribution	73,148	133,942
Textiles, clothing & footwear	73,345	77,345
Mining & quarrying	71,800	81,800
Metal goods	47,450	54,750
Paper, print & publishing	40,250	55,750
Vehicles	14,620	15,205
Timber & furniture	9,750	9,750

Note: The figures are compiled from an analysis of the accounts of the 3,000 largest UK quoted companies prepared and published by the Labour Research Group, an independent organisation affiliated to the Labour Party.

Not only does the City collectively give to the Tory Party amounts which, though small in total, are large in the context of corporate donations, but individual companies in the City also pay substantially more than their counterparts in industry. Table 6.2 shows which companies gave the largest corporate donations to the Tory Party in the election year of 1983. Only 16 companies gave more than £40,000, and of these five were City firms: British and Commonwealth Shipping, Consolidated Goldfields, Willis Faber, Sedgwick, and European Ferries, which at that time owned a merchant bank, Singer and Friedlander.

In contrast, few contributions have been directed elsewhere than to the Tory Party in recent years, and certainly none have gone to Labour, though Lord Lever did establish a bridgehead in the 1970s to a few city personalities – Sir Leslie Murphy of Schroders and Charles (now Lord) Williams, then with Barings, notable among them.

Table 6.2 Conservative Party largest corporate donors, 1983 (£)

British & Commonwealth Shipping	94,050
Hanson Trust	80,000
Racal	75,000
European Ferries	60,000
Plessey	55,000
London & Northern	54,000
Trafalgar House	50,000
AGB Research	50,000
Consolidated Goldfields	50,000
Northern Engineering	45,000
Rank Organisation	45,000
Taylor Woodrow	44,035
United Biscuits	43,000
Trusthouse Forte	41,000
Willis Faber	40,850
Sedgwick	40,000

Table 6.3 SDP/Liberal Alliance funding by companies, 1983 (£)

Commercial Union	7,000	Alliance
General Accident	5,000	Alliance
Norwich Union	5,000	SDP
Norwich Union	5,000	Liberals
Tate & Lyle	2,500	Alliance
Vantona Viyella	2,500	SDP
John Swire	2,000	SDP
I. J. Dewhurst	1,500	SDP
Morgan Crucible	1,000	SDP/Lib
H. J. Quick	250	Liberals

Those City firms who feel that the Tory way is not the only way had by 1983 largely topped up their donations to the SDP/Liberal Alliance. But their low numbers serve only to underline how much more flows into the Tory

coffers. Table 6.3 shows the top ten donations received by
the Alliance in the election year of 1983. The total at just
over £30,000 was less than the £35,000 the Tory Party
received from just one City source, Royal Insurance, and
less than a third of the £94,000 it obtained from the biggest
City donor, British and Commonwealth Shipping. It should
be noted, however, that it was the City which provided the
major contributors to Alliance funds, with three insurance
companies and two City-oriented traders, Tate and Lyle
and Swire, in the list.

Representation at Westminster

With the City's enthusiasm for political donations it might
be expected also to be well represented at Westminster.
But just as the motivation for the political contributions is
vague, so too is the City's commitment to political life. Few
city figures bother to become MPs. Some like Brian Williamson of Gerrard and National, the chairman of the
London International Financial Futures Exchange, try
when they are relatively young, but defer the ambition as
they move up the City ladder, because colleagues in the
City have little patience with those who take time off from
making money to pursue a political career. Some like Sir
Peter Tapsell, a stockbroker with James Capel, successfully combine mornings in the City with afternoons and even-
ings in the House,[10] but they are few and far between.
Normally a seat at Westminster spells the end of a City
career, while a career at Westminster, unless it is spectacular, is rarely seen as sufficient qualification for an
important role in the City. This shortage of candidates and
commitment means few from a City background attain
high office – the closest contact in recent times being Nigel
Lawson and he was a financial journalist, which hardly
counts. Most people in the City remain both ignorant of
and impatient with the minutiae of political wrangles.
Their interest begins and ends with concern at the effect
election uncertainty or government mistakes are likely to
have on the stock market or the foreign-exchange market.
  The merchant banks do, however, position themselves

discreetly to ensure that they have political connections.
The old Conservative Party was drawn from the same class
background, and many City families had members in the
House of Lords or connections with members of the House
of Commons. As the Conservative Party became less overt-
ly elitist with the election of Edward Heath as leader in
1965, they set about broadening their contacts by providing discreet employment to young Tory hopefuls whom
they find in the private offices of Ministers. They give them
a spell in the City hoping, if not to capture their loyalties,
at least to forge a contact which will be useful in future
years. Several junior ministers of the Thatcher Government of the mid-1980s served their time in the City in this
way. Norman Lamont, a Financial Secretary to the Treasury, worked for a spell in Rothschilds after cutting his
teeth in the Tory Research Department. John MacGregor,
once a Treasury Minister and later Minister of Agricul-
ture, was recruited to Hill Samuel from the private offices
of Edward Heath.

Jobs for retired Ministers and backbenchers

A more obvious contact takes place at boardroom level, and
the City has always been quick to snap up retired senior
Tories, or those temporarily out of office, to fill a non-
executive directorship and use their political experience
for the good of the firm. The list of former politicians and
civil servants in the City makes impressive reading, and
more than confirms the fact that relationships between
Whitehall-Westminster and the City depend heavily on the
movement of people, albeit that the movement is one way.

Retired Chancellors of the Exchequer are naturally
popular. Reginald Maudling, a former Chancellor and
Home Secretary in the Macmillan era, found consolation in
a managing directorship at Kleinwort Benson after losing
the battle for the Tory leadership in 1965 to Edward
Heath. His successor as Chancellor, Anthony, later Lord,
Barber became Chairman of Standard Chartered Bank,
and his chief secretary, Tom Boardman, took a peerage and
ultimately became successor to Robin Leigh Pemberton as

120 CITY WITHIN A STATE

Chairman of the National Westminster bank. John Nott moved from Warburgs into politics and rose to Defence Secretary, before returning as Sir John to become chairman of Lazards. Christopher Chataway, a junior Minister in the Heath Government, became managing director of Orion Royal Bank, a Canadian controlled merchant bank. Other political names to play the boardroom stakes, some more actively than others, include Lord Erroll and Lord Aldington, James Prior, a director of the Norwich Union insurance group when out of office between 1974 and 1979, and Geoffrey Rippon, an active chairman of the Britannia Arrow fund management group in the 1980s.

Representation is thin on the Labour side, however. Labour politicians, even former Prime Ministers, find access to City boardrooms significantly less assured. Ex-Prime Minister Lord Wilson was offered no City directorships which he chose to accept, while the best Mr, now Sir James, Callaghan could achieve was an association with Sir Julian Hodge's Commercial Bank of Wales, which is hardly front-line stuff. But another fared rather better. Roy Jenkins, one of the founders of the SDP and a former Labour Home Secretary and Chancellor as well as President of the EEC Commission, was invited to join the board of Morgan Grenfell.

Denis Healey, a distinguished if unpopular Chancellor, has no directorships, while another Minister from the Wilson era, John Stonehouse, actually became the centre of a major City scandal which resulted in his imprisonment. Edmund Dell, President of the Board of Trade under Callaghan, had a turbulent and unhappy stint as chairman and chief executive of Guinness Peat, a commodity trading and merchant banking group, in the early 1980s.

There are also superficially extensive links between backbench MPs and the City according to the register of MPs' interests. It underlines the fact that the bulk of MPs go from Westminster to the City, rather than vice versa. With just a handful of exceptions in stockbroking and merchant banking, they are usually employed as consultants or directors to make use of their parliamentary connections. They are not City people who have gone to represent the City's case in the House of Commons. The list shows that 10 MPs had links with accountancy firms, though in most cases this was because they were themselves qualified accountants, nine with banking organisations, eight with merchant banks, seven with stockbrokers, and 16 with insurance companies. There is some double counting in these numbers, however.

The most prolific link between the City and Westminster is through Lloyd's of London, the insurance market, with 54 MPs members of the market. But again this statistic does not imply any knowledge of the City, or any extensive connections, for membership of Lloyd's at this level is simply a means of capital investment, not a place of work. In only a handful of cases have working members of Lloyd's become MPs.

Jobs for the Civil Service

In addition to the movement of politicians, the City and the Civil Service both recruit strongly from the same social classes – increasingly so as the City has been forced to expand recruitment beyond its narrow bands of family and friends. As a consequence there is a considerable interchange of personnel between the two, either on a full-time basis or on a series of secondments specifically designed to increase contacts and breadth of vision.

As the salaries in the City escalated, and the demand for intelligent people as well as those with contacts increased, poaching of staff from the Civil Service rose dramatically. On top of the other demands the growth of privatisation work led to a demand in merchant banks for people who understood the Whitehall machine, and several senior civil servants followed the lead of Gerry Grimstone, the leading expert in the Treasury on privatisation, who moved to Schroders, into the private sector. In the four years up to and including 1983 almost 500 senior civil servants applied for and were almost all granted permission to quit Whitehall for private business, much of it in the City.

As the decade progressed the trend increased. But not everyone found the transition easy. Kate Mortimer, a ris-

ing star in the Treasury, who moved to Rothschilds, found
the City looked on career women far less liberally than did
the Civil Service, and it was only when she agreed to a
secondment to the Securities and Investments Board as it
was being set up in 1986 that her career began to blossom
again.

Retiring mandarins have also followed in their political
masters' footsteps. They are required to obtain prior clearance from a Scrutiny Committee headed by former Labour
Chief Secretary to the Treasury, Lord Diamond, but this is
rarely withheld. Former head of the Civil Service Douglas
Allen, as Lord Croham, became head of merchant bank
Guinness Mahon. Sir Adam Ridley, after service in the
Foreign office and Treasury, became director of the Conservative Research Department before becoming an executive director of Hambros. Sir Peter Carey, once head of the
Department of Industry, can be found at Morgan Grenfell.

Alan Lord, a Second Secretary at the Treasury, was
recruited to join Dunlop as chief executive in what turned
out to be a singularly ill-fated appointment. After Dunlop
was taken over he found another City post as chief executive of Lloyd's of London, while John Lippett, a Deputy
Secretary at the Department of Industry, joined GEC – on
that occasion after the agreement of GEC's competitors
had been sought and given. Lord Roll, who as Eric Roll had
been a key civil servant under Prime Minister Harold
Wilson, joined Warburgs and became joint chairman.

Some eyebrows were raised when Mr Heath's Man Fri-
day in Whitehall, Sir William Armstrong, moved directly
from heading the Civil Service to the chairmanship of
Midland Bank; and still more when the Secretary to the
Cabinet, Sir John, now Lord, Hunt went off to head the
London board of the Banque Nationale de Paris – until in
due course he revealed that he had been headhunted for
the job by none other than the Governor of the Bank of
England. Elsewhere Sir Nicholas Henderson, Britain's
ambassador to the United States during the Falklands
war, became a director of Hambros in 1983, and Sir
Michael Palliser, a former head of the Foreign Office, became chairman of Samuel Montagu.

Conclusion

If, to use the old cliché, the Church of England is the Tory Party at prayer, the City is certainly the Tory Party at work. But just as the barbs thrown at the Thatcher Government by turbulent clerics have shown the tension in relations between Church and State, so the squabbles between the Bank of England and the Treasury, and between Tory Ministers at Westminster and City investing institutions, show that this relationship is also sometimes torn by dissent, and is never easy. The City and the Tory Party may ultimately count on each other as allies in time of war, but in time of peace they pursue their own interests, regardless of the effect on the other side.

It is easy to suspect that, because of the finance the City provides for the Tory Party, because of the lobbying role of the Bank of England, because of the interchange of people and jobs, and because of the close personal contacts and the common social background between the two, the City exerts a considerable influence on Whitehall and also on Westminster. But the reality is rather different. There is certainly a continual and continuing contact between senior civil servants and politicians and senior City figures at informal lunches where politicians are frequent guests, and at official and semi-official dinners. But generally the City seems to feel it can keep its political lines open by the simple expedient of giving jobs to senior civil servants when they approach retirement, or to senior politicians when they are out of office, or by employing them as consultants and contacts.

It is a view which sums up the City's continued naiveté in political matters. Because it has always worked on connections and contacts as a means of doing business and getting things done, it assumes that is all it needs to do in Westminster and Whitehall. Its practitioners have never really come to terms with the realities of political life in which politicians will not only say one thing and do another but, which is worse in the City's eyes, accept the hospitality of a merchant banker or broker's lunch table, and still refuse to accept the arguments presented over the port.

The City has ways in which it can and does get its way
and, as we saw from the Montagu Norman era, if it chooses
it can make it virtually impossible for a government to
function. Although City institutions support the Tories
financially, they cannot be relied upon to do what a Tory
government wants them or asks them to do. Mrs Thatcher
should have realised this before she launched the Channel
Tunnel project on the assumption that City fund managers
would share her vision, and automatically come up with
the thousands of millions of pounds needed to make the
venture possible. The project missed its deadline even in
raising the first £250 million and the Prime Minister had
to lean on the Governor of the Bank of England, who in
turn leant heavily on the City's institutions, reminding
them of the political dangers which would follow if the
project collapsed at its first, very minor financial hurdle.
As a consequence it just scraped home.

Much earlier in her career, however, she had faced an
even greater challenge from the City when, like Labour
Chancellor Denis Healey before her in 1976, she was confronted by a buyer's strike – City jargon for a refusal by the
investing institutions to put any more money into a specific stock or government bond. This happens when the
financial institutions in the City are so disenchanted with
government policy that they refuse to buy any more government stock. The idea is not deliberately to make it
impossible for government to function, but that is the practical effect if the strike is sustained.

The Thatcher Government was struck in this way in
September/October 1981, and again in July 1984, and was
thereby faced by the City with a cruel dilemma – either to
change its policies so that the buyers felt happy to buy the
stock at the current level of interest rates, or to try to stare
out the markets and impress them with its resolution. In
both cases the Conservative Government successfully
stared out the market – an option which had not been
available to Denis Healey; his only way out had been to
call in the IMF and obtain a loan, the conditions of which
entailed a major change of policy.

Normally policy is modified long before it reaches this

level, and the Governor of the Bank of England at his
weekly meetings with the Chancellor is expected to give an
early warning of such potential problems. In this way the
City ultimately imposes its will on the government. The
Governor may get short shrift when lobbying in Whitehall
on the general run of City affairs, but when he reads the
riot act in Downing Street, as Richardson was wont to do,
and says that he refuses to be answerable for the consequences if ministers or the Treasury attempt to resist market
pressures, then even the strongest Chancellors, regardless
of party, are likely to yield. In political terms this means
that ultimately the government must do what the City
wants or pay an unacceptably high price in the form of
high interest rates and currency crises. The reality is that
the government needs the City to pay its bills, and has to
accept the City on its own apolitical terms.

7

The City and Foreign Policy

In the heyday of the Empire, Britain's military suprema-
cy was matched by its financial might, and in the same
way that the British Navy ruled the oceans of the world, so
too the British banker controlled the financial currents of
the world. Thus it was that the Duc de Richelieu, French
soldier statesman and politician, thundered more than 150
years ago, 'There are six great powers in Europe – England, France, Russia, Austria, Prussia and the Baring
Brothers', Barings being the leading bank in the City of
London at the time.

A rival power

Richelieu's observation contained another truth, however
– namely, that the power of the City on the international
scene in his day was distinct and separate from the power
of the state. The City had its own foreign policy. That much
was apparent to the politicians and statesmen of the
nineteenth century, and it is one of the problems of the
twentieth that the current generation of British politicians
has quite failed to appreciate the extent to which it remains true today. They may think they dictate the part
Britain plays in foreign affairs, but their power is largely a
sham, whereas the City can and does still exert a very real

influence – usually on the same side as the government, but occasionally in direct opposition to its policies.

The City has become highly skilled over the years at creating the impression that it will do what it wants to do rather than what the government wants it to do. The City's clear message – that money knows neither politics nor frontiers – has led to its being used by all, and trusted by a surprisingly large number of governments which are nominally at loggerheads with Whitehall.

The extent to which the City's bankers remain discreet financial advisers to the world's governments remains one of the Square Mile's best kept secrets. British merchant banks do a huge but largely secret business advising foreign governments on everything from one-off deals on the best way to finance an infrastructure project to detailed political and economic input which gives them a hand, though they would never admit it, directly in the running of the nation. Information on the extent of this influence is shadowy, but it is known, for example, that Barings is the adviser to the monetary authority of Saudi Arabia, which, thanks to its oil wealth, is one of the world's richest nations and a key power in the politics of the Middle East.

Barings never talks about this role, but rival merchant bankers claim that it has built up a close understanding with the Saudi leaders and has played a key part in analysing the likely economic effects of various oil market strategies – thereby enabling the Saudi leaders to know how much they can afford to cut production, and how long they can afford low oil prices. Barings' advice was therefore central to the Saudi position in the tortuous negotiations among the world's oil producers throughout the mid-1980s, when they adjusted production to manipulate the price of oil to try to force producers to agree on production quotas.

Several other merchant banks have similar links.[1] Schroders is a key adviser to the Singapore Government on its privatisation programme, as is N.M. Rothschild to Jamaica under Prime Minister Edward Seaga. Rothschilds also advises the investment arm of the Singapore Government – not actually managing the $15 billion or so it has,

but providing the strategic thinking which gives a
framework to its investment policies. Schroders advises a
number of central banks in addition to Singapore, and is
deeply involved with Venezuela, while Samuel Montagu
has contacts with the central bank of the Dominican Re-
public, and with the governments of Sierra Leone, Jamaica
and Zambia. The merchant banking arm of Lloyds is deeply involved with South America, as a result of Lloyds now
owning the former Bank of London and South America,
while Morgan Grenfell is adviser to a string of African
countries, including Zambia and Kenya, and does a huge
amount of government consultancy work.

Much of this work is routine financial advice, but it can
also be economically and politically controversial – when,
for example, the British merchant banks give advice to
Third World debtor nations which is basically aimed at
getting them off the debt hook. One of their number described their work thus:[2]

> Just as commercial banks were keen to lend in the first
> place, so they are keen to extort what they can when a
> country is on its beam ends. . . . The puny forces of the
> central bank are not equipped to stand up to the chappies
> from New York. We are in the second row, whispering advice
> over the client's shoulder, making sure he isn't conned.

Naturally enough the international commercial banks do
not take kindly to the merchant banks – most of whom
have no money at risk, having written off or sold at a
discount their own Third World loans – slipping in through
the back door to tell the debtor how best to keep the other
bankers and the IMF at bay.

Sometimes the British banks work alone, sometimes in
tandem with a New York investment bank. One multina-
tional alliance consists of Lehman Brothers (now Shearson
Lehman) of New York, Lazard Frères of New York and
Paris, and S.G. Warburg of London. They were in Indone-
sia in 1975, competing for the contract to sort out Pertamina, the state oil corporation. Since then, collaborating
rather than in competition, they have worked for Panama,
Turkey, Gabon, Zaire, Sri Lanka, and Costa Rica.

The influence these banks have today is inevitably less than that enjoyed by their ancestors. With the sophisticated communications of the twentieth century, governments can go to any of half a dozen financial centres to raise money when they have exhausted the ability of their native inhabitants to pay any more in taxes. In the nineteenth century they did not have this option, and London was the only international capital market. London alone had a currency that was internationally acceptable, and the political stability and military might to reassure borrowers and depositors. It was therefore vitally important to all but the most powerful countries like the emerging United States, which allowed some of its states to default, that countries maintained their credit rating in London. This did not mean that they had to be on good terms with the British Government; Austria, Prussia, France and Russia frequently were not. But it did mean that they had to be on good terms with the City's bankers and money lenders who judged creditworthiness by the ability and willingness of the client country to pay the interest on the loans, not by what it did with the money.

It is hard now fully to appreciate the scale on which Britain was banker to the world, the modern equivalent of the International Monetary Fund, the World Bank and the New York and London capital markets all rolled into one. And just as the Americans as the main contributors to these institutions today try to use the IMF and World Bank to support specific objectives within their foreign policy – the loans to Egypt after the Camp David accords with Israel being an example – so the British Government, through its informal and family links with the City's bankers, used British wealth as a discreet arm of foreign policy.

Banker to Europe

Nineteenth-century Britain was, in spite of Parliamentary reform, still largely governed by members of the aristocracy and that same aristocracy was infiltrated by those of the newly affluent bankers who invested heavily in achieving the status of landed gentry. Contrary to the present day, there was a considerable commonality of thinking between the City and Westminster and a regular unofficial interchange of views throughout the period. In addition, the Bank of England could be relied upon when consulted to give an 'official' City view on world events.

It is not surprising therefore that the habit grew up then, and still persists, for the bankers' wealth to be used when an overt British intervention might have been counterproductive. The rewards came in the form of peerages. All the leading merchant bankers established dynasties in the Victorian era. Most notably, Lord Rothschild became a rare Jewish member of the House of Lords – an event still commemorated in a painting on the directors' floor of the bank.

All the big banks were involved – the Barings, the Schroders, the Rothschilds, and the Brandts – but it was a relative newcomer, Hambros, which stole the limelight. Hambros Bank came on to the international stage through work in Italy and Scandinavia. Hambros came to finance the unification of Italy, having won the confidence of Cavour by helping him restore the creditworthiness of his province, Sardinia. In the years that followed while Garibaldi won the military victories and Mazzini was the populist diplomat, it was the quiet political skill of Cavour which provided the grand design to make it all happen, and Hambros which raised the bulk of the money.

A concurrent example occurred when the Prussians invaded Schleswig Holstein, at the base of the Danish peninsula, in 1848. The Danes fought off the challenge but at great cost, and in 1850 the Government was forced to seek a foreign loan. Hambros already had strong links with Scandinavia. One of the clan, Joseph Hambro, had been born in Copenhagen in 1780, and family members were already official Court bankers to Denmark, Norway, and Sweden. So it was to them that the Danish Government turned. In 1850 Hambros raised a loan of £800,000 in London and a grateful government made Carl Joachim Hambro a Danish Baron in 1851. Today the head of the Hambro family still bears this inherited title.

Nor was this a one-off success. Eleven years later in 1862

Carl Joachim Hambro informally introduced Prince Wilhelm of Denmark, who was making a chance visit to London, to officials who were then prominent in the Greek Government and looking for a replacement for the unpopular King Otto. As a direct result of this introduction Wilhelm was nominated to the Crown of Greece the following year, and Hambros not unnaturally became the fiscal agent – or adviser – to the Greek Government.

The success of the City in attracting bankers from all over the world meant that the determined borrower could always find someone with a sympathetic ear. The sorely pressed French discovered this when, following the shattering defeat by the invading Prussians at Sedan in September 1870, and with Paris under siege, they sounded out City bankers for a loan. The leading merchant banks had strong German ancestry, however. Barings and the Schroders were of German origin, the Rothschilds were from Austria, and this, coupled with the fact that France was clearly heading for defeat, meant the requests were shunned, until one J. S. Morgan, the founder of Morgan Grenfell, became involved. He was newly arrived in London from New York and anxious to build up his business, so he agreed to raise £10 million. It was a struggle but he did it, and as it was a vast sum of money for those times the transaction established Morgan in the City.

The ramifications of the loan were far greater than the making of a young man's name, however brilliant. Siding with the defeated French fostered the climate of reconciliation and rapprochement between Britain and France after centuries of conflict and was to culminate in the Entente Cordiale between the two countries. This in turn led to the British entering the First World War as allies of the French in 1914.

An arm of foreign policy

In the nineteenth century the City had a clear ability to separate finance from politics, but it also had a more shadowy ability to run the two in tandem. Foreign governments who were customers of the City could see incon-

sistency at Westminster, and match it against a consisten-
cy of purpose in the City, with the result that they came to
believe in the City as the real heart of British interests.

This attitude still exists today. Witness the willingness
of the oil-rich Arab nations to deposit the bulk of their
surplus oil revenues in Britain rather than in any other
financial centre, in spite of frequent clashes over decades
with British political interests. And the Sultan of Brunei
found, when asked personally by Prime Minister Margaret
Thatcher to maintain several billion pounds of deposits in
Britain at a time of sterling weakness, that the depositing
of money can also build up a considerable store of political
capital as well.

The apparent detachment of the City can also help the
politicians. It was a Bank of England official Sir Kit
McMahon, not a politician, who played a key role in the
release of the American hostages held in Iran throughout
1980. As mentioned earlier, though the British Government was suspect, the Iranians, the Algerian intermediaries and the Americans trusted the Bank to handle the
vast sums of money which needed to be transferred to bring
about an end to the crisis.[3] Thus it was the Bank, and not
the Foreign Office, which hammered out the details and
executed the financial transactions which enabled the hostages to be freed.

Relations were not always so harmonious, however, and
the interests of the Government and the City do not always
so clearly coincide, as the experience of the international
debt crisis shows. The City's interest has been in solving
the crisis, or at least keeping it at bay so that the structure
of the financial community could be maintained. But such
a broad policy has been at odds with the narrower interests
of the Government and the foreign policy it wished to
pursue, specifically when, as happened in the 1980s, two of
the most troublesome debtors to emerge were Poland and
Argentina.

Argentina. After the Falklands war in 1982 it became
apparent that the new civilian Government of Argentina
was teetering on the brink of a major debt default which

could have put at risk as much as $50 billion of international loans and dealt a major, and possibly catastrophic, blow to the world banking system. The custodians of the world financial system, the central banks, were naturally desperate to avoid this and the US Federal Reserve Board and the Bank of England secretly worked out a rescue package, which promised to stave off the default by injecting massive new loans into the economy and postponing or re-scheduling the repayments due on those already granted. The British clearing banks were then invited to join in the rescue plan. They had all been among the original major international lenders to Argentina, and vast amounts of their money were at risk.

In spite of these links, however, it was a sensitive matter when Lloyds and the other big British banks were asked by the Bank of England to pump rescue capital into a country with which only a few weeks previously Britain had been at war, and which had not officially renounced its claim on the Falkland Islands which had provoked the hostilities. In her public utterances the Prime Minister appeared to be furious at the sight of the City coming to the aid of the enemy, and the matter was clearly a major political embarrassment. Privately, however, it is hard to believe that the Government was not as relieved as the rest of the world that a way was being sought to shore up Argentina and avoid international financial collapse. The City refused to be cowed into submission by the political storm; the British banks were well aware that if they did not take part they might destroy the whole rescue operation and bring an international financial crisis down on their heads. Such a crisis, with banks falling like ninepins, was an inconceivable price to pay, whatever the wishes of the Government.

They were anxious, however, to prepare their ground carefully before being drawn into a confrontation, and they therefore asked the Bank of England for guidance. Anxious as ever to preserve the health and reputation of the City, the Bank urged them to participate in the re-financing. In its efforts to put pressure on the banks, the Government turned on the Bank of England, but found it unyielding. Governor Richardson insisted to Downing Street that the

banks be allowed to proceed with the package, and once
they were assured of his support, they went ahead and
joined the rescue syndicate. They stated publicly by their
actions, as clearly as if it had been proclaimed from the
floor of the House of Commons, that the interests of the
City and the international financial community took pre-
cedence over the British Government's conduct of foreign
policy.

Poland.   British banks had been major lenders to Poland
but, whereas in the South American case it was the American banks generally who took the initiative and brought
the British banks in on the back of their rescheduling, in
Poland's case many more of the British banks were lead
managers – in other words, they were in the front line.
They had put the loan deals together in the first place, in
the rush in the mid- to late-1970s to recycle the oil surplus
generated by the OPEC nations, and they frequently had
retained the major slice of these Polish loans on their own
books rather than syndicated them to other overseas
banks. They also, not unimportantly, had the responsibility in the eyes of the world banking community to sort
things out.

In achieving this the bankers were severely hampered
by the rise of the Polish trade union, Solidarity, because
the stronger the union became the more it demanded a
better domestic deal for the Poles and the less money there
was to pay the interest on foreign loans. No one in the City
was insensitive enough to express the thought publicly,
but the rise of the Polish protest movement was a cause for
considerable unease, as it was seen to heighten rather than
alleviate the problems of that tottering economy.

The affair came into the open, however, with the military takeover of December 1981. The British Government,
prodded by the Reagan Administration, agreed to a trade
embargo in protest against the imposition of martial law,
and in an attempt to secure the release of the Solidarity
leaders who had been rounded up. To the City's bankers,
however, the military takeover was the signal they had
been waiting for. Here was a strong regime with which

they could deal, and unlike its predecessor, it was a regime which could deliver what it promised. The call for an embargo was ignored and the teams of international bankers, generally under British chairmanship, pressed quickly ahead with talks aimed at rescheduling a large chunk of the $30 billion of Poland's debts, re-financing the economy and going a considerable way towards underpinning the new regime by helping it to avoid economic collapse.

The Government knew what was going on but it was the prisoner of its own rhetoric in support of sanctions and its policy of public support for the United States. Privately it accepted that the danger of international financial collapse if Poland slid into default was far more damaging to the country than the further repression of Polish liberties – unlike 1939, when Britain went to war over the threat to that country posed by Nazi Germany.

Out of the hands of politicians

Such action did mean, however, that the decisions affecting real British interests – in this case the avoidance of global financial collapse to preserve the nation's prosperity – were taken by unelected and anonymous bankers. The decision on whether the Polish state should survive or be allowed to collapse economically was taken by men whose primary concern was to try to get as much as possible of their money back, and who wanted stability regardless of social or political cost.

The City is therefore more than just another lobby competing for parliamentary attention and a share of the nation's resources. Throughout the debt crisis it represented the real British interest more truly than the Government did, and the Government recognised this fact by delegating the international effort to contain the crisis to the Bank of England. It was therefore Gordon Richardson as Governor of the Bank who activated the Basle Club – the group of international central bankers – to co-ordinate policy to contain the crisis, and the extent to which the crisis was managed was largely due to his intellectual toughness and diplomatic skills. His success in pulling off such a spectacularly difficult task should not lead one to overlook the fact that he was not an elected representative; nevertheless, he and his successor had effective control over the most crucial foreign policy issue to affect Britain in the 1980s. It is as well for the authority of the Government that the debt crisis, and the role of the bankers vis à vis the politicians, was rarely discussed in public.

The degree of control that any government can exercise over its financial community has decreased dramatically with the growth of global markets, the increase of international currency flows, and the breaking down of barriers to restrict the movement of capital. Not only has the City's world role run well ahead of the ability of the Government to keep it in check, but all the indicators are that the trend will continue. The more currencies, capital and interest rates become influenced by global trends and worldwide speculative movements, the less an individual government can remain master of its own destiny. To the extent that the bankers in the City can understand these movements, and channel them to their own advantage they will do so. If in the process they run foul of the perceived interests of the country as articulated by the Foreign Office or the politicians of the day, it is unlikely to deflect them from the pursuit of profit.

8
The City and Industry

'The Stock Exchange is first and foremost a market for industrial capital', according to Chairman of the Stock Exchange, Sir Nicholas Goodison.[1] 'The Stock Exchange could not exist without industry. Our whole philosophy is to be close to it.'[2] If that is how the Stock Exchange should be judged, however, then it has to address the question of its responsibility for British industrial performance, and why, even in a year like 1986 when £14 billion of capital was raised for industry on the Stock Exchange,[3] generations of entrepreneurs have complained of how difficult it is to raise capital in Britain. In spite of, or because of, its highly developed financial system, it has been harder to get backing for a business idea in Britain than in other developed countries.

The British system, with its emphasis on the Stock Exchange, contrasts with that of Japan or the continental European countries, where stock markets have traditionally played a minor role in the provision of finance. Would-be industrialists in those countries relied, usually successfully, on the commercial banks for support, and found in those banks people who understood and sensibly evaluated their ideas.

Britain in contrast had the worst of both worlds. The City traditionally attracted the brightest of the recruits in

banking, leaving the clearing banks understaffed and ill-
equipped to carry out an imaginative lending role on the
scale required. But though the Stock Exchange and City
firms attracted the talent, they misdirected it. Inherited
wealth and the amateur traditions inherent in the British
public school culture created a risk-averse society with the
City as its hub; the emphasis was on preserving fortunes
rather than on fostering the creation of new ones. The
investment policies of the City put safety and modest
yields before high risk and high return. The result was
that the City failed to finance the creation of new
businesses on anything like the scale the country needed,
and this explains, at least in part, why British Governments occasionally try to bridge the gap – usually with
disastrous results like the De Lorean Motor project in
Northern Ireland.

The culture gap

Judged by the standards obtaining abroad, City financiers
appear to be remote both geographically and intellectually
from industry. This remoteness was tacitly acknowledged
by the Stock Exchange in 1986 when it set up an Industrial
Policy Unit designed to organise exchange visits and foster
dialogue and understanding between the financial and industrial sectors. It was seen again during and after a stor-
my annual conference of the Confederation of British Industry in November 1986 during which the City was widely attacked for its short-term thinking. The CBI subsequently set up a committee to try to quantify the reasons
for the divide and take steps to reduce them.

In the United States the venture capital industry has
been based in the industrial heartlands where the companies were likely to be formed. In Britain almost all
financial houses have been located in the City, which
proved such a magnet for the talented that there was very
little sophisticated independent financial expertise available in the industrial areas, where the financiers might be
expected to have an understanding of the industrial culture. Nor did City-based merchant banks believe it made

economic sense to have regional offices.[4] Though some,
notably Singer and Friedlander, tried it, others thought
there was not enough range and depth of work in provincial centres to give their staff the experience they needed to
progress in the bank. This meant that a provincial posting
was likely to be seen as a backwater, and that decisions
taken at local level were often overturned at head office.

Nor did the City firms compensate by hiring their own
industrial and technical experts. Again, in marked contrast to the US investment houses, it was rare even in the
early 1980s to find in-house technical experts in any of the
London merchant banks capable of evaluating sophisticated industrial projects and ideas. Indeed, they frequently
went to the opposite extreme and patronised the potential
entrepreneurs to a degree which alienated them from the
City for the remainder of their industrial lives.

Though the matter was extensively debated in the
1980s, the need to channel funds into industry and Britain's failure to do so adequately was not a new problem. In
1931 the Macmillan Committee on Finance and Industry[5]
discussed the failure of UK financial institutions to provide risk capital for new businesses, particularly those
hoping to use new technologies. This led to the Bank of
England and the four major clearing banks launching the
Industrial and Commercial Finance Corporation, ICFC, to
bridge what was by then known as the Macmillan gap.
ICFC, now part of Investors in Industry, 3i, grew to be one
of the largest providers of venture capital in the world.

On its own, however, it failed to solve the problem. In
1959 the Radcliffe Committee on the Working of the
Monetary System,[6] and in the late 1970s the Wilson Committee to Review the Functioning of the Financial
Institutions,[7] returned to the same field, and examined the
workings of the UK financial institutions to find out why it
was that Britain failed to create the right climate for new
business. The majority of the Wilson Committee came to
the conclusion that the City was not at fault;[8] it found that
the problem was not shortage of cash but shortage of ideas
worth backing, and saw no need for the City to be more
active in seeking out ideas, nor more encouraging to those

who came to it. Yet the validity of this judgement was
called into question some years later by both the Governor
of the Bank of England, Robin Leigh-Pemberton, and the
Chancellor of the Exchequer, Nigel Lawson. The Governor
was forced in 1984 to tell the City that it should be 'not
only responsive to industry's needs, but it has also got to
positively [sic] promote industrial development and
change'.[9] And Nigel Lawson told a Stock Exchange audi-
ence that there was little doubt that the growth of new
businesses had been hampered by the existence of the
so-called equity gap. It had been 'notoriously difficult to
raise even very small sums of equity – say between £20,000
and £50,000', he claimed.[10]

Remoteness is not just a physical matter, there is intellectual remoteness too. Though Lawson did not say so,
failures of this kind have been an inevitable consequence
of the nature of the City. At least until recent times, its
people had generally received a classical rather than a
technical education, and many were cushioned from economic realities by inherited wealth. As a result, they were
socially, politically and culturally at odds with the rest of
the country, and with the entrepreneurs who did not come
from the same narrow social background.

This was occasionally recognised. In 1985 the Secretary
of State for Wales, the Rt Hon. Nicholas Edwards MP,
spoke of a 'huge chasm' between the City and the industrial areas of Britain. He described how many people still
saw Wales as a country heavily dependent on the traditional coal and steel industries, ravaged by industrial derelic-
tion and lacking in vitality to encourage change. This
perception is typically prevalent in the City of London,
where the bulk of the financial institutions capable of
disbursing funds to help the development of the Welsh
economy have their headquarters.[11] Edwards hinted at a
further problem, when he talked of the hostile reception
entrepreneurs received when they went for funds.

> It is the entrepreneur who has to try to bridge the gap going
> to the City to offices away from the action to explain in an
> alien and sometimes hostile climate the potential for the
> project.

What made the problem unique to Britain was its cultural rather than its commercial origin. This is best illustrated by the fact that the City did take risks and did invest in start-ups and new ventures. But in the 1970s and 1980s it preferred these ventures to be located in the United States and to a lesser extent the Far East, rather than in Britain. The reason was the City's belief that the American culture was a genuinely capitalist culture, where entrepreneurs red in tooth and claw would work hard to make investment ideas work. Though they may not practise it themselves, City investment managers admire this culture, and consider that an investment in the United States is more likely to be successful than an equivalent investment in the UK. They have therefore been prepared to invest in the US venture for a lower return than they would want to see from a potential UK business, to compensate for the greater risk inherent in the UK venture. This cultural paradox was one of the causes of the phenomenon noted by the Wilson Committee – that the cost of capital was higher in Britain than among its competitors.

City investment managers generally are sceptical of Britain's entrepreneurial culture, and they have not felt confident in backing the general run of British businessmen. Robin Leigh-Pemberton noted the bias, in the Bank of England's typically elliptical way. Explaining the reluctance of City institutions to invest in new industry he said:[12]

> Its sentiment towards big new departures is likely to be based on an amalgam of the track record of UK industry as a whole when it embarks on such new ventures and on its assessment of the management of the company.

Moreover, many people in the City, and even more in industry, consider that the role of supplying start-up capital to industry rests with the commercial banks, not with the specialists in the Square Mile, and that any shortcoming in this area therefore lies at the door of the High Street clearing banks. These banks are criticised, however, for being excessively cautious. Bank managers are conditioned not to take risks, and not to be daring and innova-

tive. They are penalised disproportionately in the promotion stakes if one of their loans goes sour. Instead of encouraging them to lend aggressively so that they have
enough winners to compensate for the losers, the clearing
bank philosophy has been to avoid mistakes. American
banks in contrast are much more willing to help new
businesses, while German and Japanese banks forge much
closer and longer-term links with their clients. These are
significant reasons for the continued vitality of these economies compared to that of the UK.

There is substance in this criticism. British commercial
banks are among the largest in the world, though the
Japanese in the 1980s overtook them in sheer size, and the
Americans have a comparable global spread. But because
they expanded with the Empire, they have tended to be
trade-related banks, with a lending tradition which aimed
at financing trade transactions. With the exception of the
Midland, they have a much shorter and less well developed
tradition of industrial lending. The two-thirds of UK bank
lending to non-banks (£120 billion) which went to industry
in 1985 compares unfavourably with the volume of bank
credit available in the USA and Japan, where domestic
bank lending was respectively eight times and six times
what it was in the UK.[13] Although these economies operate on a much larger scale, the figures to suggest that bank
lending plays a relatively more important role in them
than it does in Britain. This in turn suggests that the UK
is a relative difficult place in which to raise an industrial
loan, despite its sophisticated banking system.

New issues and capital raising

In spite of claims that the City exists for industry, or could
not exist without it, it organises such basic functions as
capital raising to meet the needs of the institutional investor rather than the users of the market.

Price and timing. The hardest part of the flotation of a
new issue is to decide at what price the shares should be
sold. Go for too much and the issue will flop; ask for too

little and it will soar high above the selling price and
appear to have been launched too cheaply. The great skill
of the issuing houses, and the reason why they justify fees
running into millions on a company of any size (the underwriting of the issue alone costing 1.25 per cent of the
proceeds), is in getting this equation right.

The City's approach to the handling of new issues has
been dismissed as inefficient and too costly by such respected figures as Stanislas Yassukovich, head of Merrill
Lynch Europe, an American who has worked more than
twenty years in the City.[14] He considers that the City's
procedure discriminates against the client company because it is constructed to ensure that the investing institutions take the minumum of risk for a disproportionate
amount of profit. American houses handle their issues in a
different way; they buy the entire issue and assume the
risk in return for a fee. As a result, share prices of new
issues seldom soar far beyond their issue price in early
dealings.

Yassukovich is not alone in this criticism. Lord King, a
leading British industrialist, the Chairman of British Airways and a close friend of Margaret Thatcher, was sufficiently sceptical about the City practice to devote his
maiden speech in the House of Lords to a plea for a different method of selling shares, and less bias in favour of the
institutional investor. He complained that the present way
of owning shares seemed obscure and unacceptable to most
people. The objective should be to reverse the downward
trend in private share ownership in UK industry and commerce, and he argued that this could be achieved by remov-
ing the mystique of share ownership and bringing the
means of acquiring shares to the High Street, particularly
by means of the building societies.[15]

The basic problem facing the issuing house at present is
that it is possible for fund managers to make or break an
issue, regardless of the merits of a company, because they
dominate the British capital markets. Fund managers
have a very strong herd instinct. They all like to invest or
disinvest at the same time, so that none can be seen to be
taking undue risks. Either they all like an issue, or they all

hate it. Normally the issuing house leans excessively on
the side of caution so that the fund manager can see that
the shares are a bargain. But it does not always work. In
spite of the high fees charged, and in spite of the acclaimed
expertise, the pricing of new issues sometimes appears
disastrously wrong.

The criticism has been particularly acute in the case of
the privatisation programme, where the early record was
so patchy that the Public Accounts Committee of the House
of Commons questioned whether the country was getting
value for money. It reviewed the privatisation policy applied to British Aerospace, Associated British Ports and
Britoil and found it erratic and unsatisfactory.[16] Treasury
officials dismiss this complaint, however, on the grounds
that the issues were deliberately under-priced for political
reasons. The aim was to ensure the success of future issues
and to encourage a wider spread of individuals owning
shares, and offering them cheaply was seen as one way to
achieve this.[17]

Parliament was not the only critic. The managing director of one public company, Aircall, described the process of
going public in the City of London as being exposed to 'the
greatest money squeezing organisation that you will ever
come across outside your wife and children and the
Mafia'.[18] He added:

> Realise that there are links upon links in the establishment
> chain which are there to give you words of comfort and
> support but squeezing you for every penny in the most soph-
> isticated ways imaginable. Realise that this establishment
> exists on charging fees. Realise that it exists on making you
> trade successfully, and realise that it only likes successes not
> failures.

The City judges new issues from the perspective of the
purchaser, not the seller. It calls an issue a success when it
gets the shares cheap and sees an immediate profit; it calls
it a failure when it appears to have paid a full price which
it cannot immediately improve upon. Whether the people
who created the business and who are now selling part of it
are happy with the issue price is relevant only to the extent

that the advisers presumably want to keep the company as a client, so that they can advise and earn fees on any future transactions, and therefore need to maintain a reasonable relationship.

Under the current system it is hard for the situation to be otherwise, as one can see from looking at the role of the broker to the issue. Brokers to small companies, which most new issues are, live by commission even in these deregulated post-Big Bang days. A flop to a broker is an issue which does not go to a 20 per cent premium.

Again, the reason is basic to the system. The broker handles the initial issue in which the shares are sold, and he makes a commission. But he does not want that to be the end of the matter; he wants to make further commissions. He therefore needs a premium in order to persuade the first generation of public holders to sell and take their profit, and to convince the second generation, new investors all, that stock is an essential part of any serious investor's portfolio. Providing enough second-generation investors come in, the price is pushed up still further and the process is repeated with the second generation selling out and the third generation coming in. And each and every sale and purchase generates a further stock market commission.

A record of dramatic upward movement on the stock market fast track means a commissions bonanza. It makes the broker's sales story much more plausible and gets this process of selling and reselling off to a flying start. But contrast this with what happens if the shares go to a discount. Then there are no dealing profits to be taken, only losses to be nursed. There is no clamour for the shares, only relief at having avoided the issue. There is no commission on secondary and tertiary sales, but a pressing need to sweeten the distinctly soured investors who bought the stock on the broker's recommendation in the first place. Institutional investors who are notably sensitive about being made to look foolish in the eyes of their trustees may even funnel other business to a rival broker as a sign of displeasure.

Having put the argument from the client's point of view,

it is only fair to concede that the City also has a case. Hill
Samuel, one of the leading merchant banks, produced an
analysis in 1986 which defined a successful new issue as
one where the shares open at a premium of between 5 and
15 per cent. The bank's head of corporate finance, Trevor
Swete, was quoted as saying that 'the ideal is that after the
first week of dealings there should be a ten per cent premium above the flotation price'.[19]

Other bankers broadly support this view. They believe
such a gain produces a price which is buoyant enough to
provide an aftermarket in the shares and generate continuing investor interest in the company sufficient to support it in issuing more shares for takeover bids or capital-
raising issues. But it must also be sufficiently close to the
issue price for the sellers not to have reason to feel
aggrieved that they have parted with their slice of the
company too cheaply.

Queuing. The British system of capital raising is also
notoriously inflexible when compared to that of the United
States. The great advantage the American financial institutions offer their clients is speed; if a company decides
it wants money it can raise it quickly and while market
conditions are favourable. In Britain this is not possible.
Absurd though it may sound, companies wishing to raise
new capital on the stock market have to join a queue.
When they get to the front of the queue, which could be
after a six to nine month delay, it may no longer be economic for them to raise the money. Alternatively, as Thames
Television experienced when it went public in 1986, the
queue was shorter than it expected and the company had to
make preparations for the issue much more rapidly than it
had intended.[20]

The reason for the queue was well intentioned enough
originally – but it has hardly stood the test of time. The
system is operated by the Government Broker, a member
of the staff of the Bank of England, so as to phase the
demands for money in an orderly way. The Bank's intention is twofold – to avoid too many companies trying to

raise capital at the same time, so that there is always enough to go round, and to ensure that companies do not mop up all the spare cash and leave nothing for the government sector .

The system discriminates against industry, however, because the Bank's two roles conflict. Its primary role is to be the government's banker and to manage the orderly sale of government debt so that Whitehall is never without its money. And government's demands frequently clash with industry's needs. The Bank therefore not only has a vested interest in putting government before industry, it has an obligation to do so. As a result, even when stock market conditions are favourable for raising new money, companies are put off to the end of the queue and this means that they do not raise capital as cheaply as they might. Consequently, British industry has relied excessively on bank overdrafts rather than equity to meet its short-term capital needs, and this in turn has made long-term investment decisions and planning considerably harder than they need be.

The procedure is inefficient in capital-raising terms and rests on a narrow and outdated perception of the stock market, as a purely domestic organisation. In fact, the modest capital needs of most British companies are well within the capacity of the new international securities houses now operating in London. They are keen to promote 'bought deals' where the securities house takes all the stock the company wishes to sell, and thereby assumes the risk inherent in the issue. But this obviously requires an acute feel for the market as well as a knowledge of the client company, and is incompatible with queueing.

The queue would be more justifiable if the need for it was self-evident, but those days have long gone. When most shares were held by individuals it was reasonable to phase demands for cash. But the bulk of shares are now held by insurance companies and pension funds which have such huge cash flows that their problem is finding places to put the money rather than finding the sums to invest. What the queue does now is artificially to restrict the amount of capital for industry which the market can absorb.

Takeover pressure

Thus the City, ostensibly the servant of industry and
commerce, has been in fact its master in many respects,
exerting a considerable influence over the British industrial structure. Availability of finance is one of the main
constraints on a company's growth, and the City is the
major source of finance. Companies which were supported
were moulded and developed along the lines they knew the
City liked and would support, and this led to a quite
different industrial pattern from those occurring in other
countries.

The City's skills made it easier for British companies to
grow by acquisition, instead of having to endure the slow
hard slog of ploughing back resources to develop their own
businesses. As a result, large companies account for a
higher proportion of national output in the United Kingdom than in any comparable country.

This has brought advantages and disadvantages. In the
retailing sector the dominance of the market by a few
highly efficient chains brought great benefits to the
consumer in the range of goods available and their
cheapness. But it also made it much easier for importers to
penetrate the UK market because by dealing with just a
few firms they can gain national distribution. The consumer benefits from these imports, but they adversely affect
British manufacturing and employment.

Britain has also been more takeover-prone than other
countries because of the heavy concentration of shareholdings in the hands of a few professional fund managers.
Most big bids have been decided by fewer than 50 fund
managers and massive efforts have been made to lobby
them and win their support.[21]

The City likes takeovers because it looks at them from
the point of view of the investor rather than the industrialist. It rates highly those companies which can show a
consistent record of fast growth in assets and earnings per
share. It is less concerned about how that growth is
achieved. In consequence, it appreciates takeover specialists who can move in to sluggish companies, prune and

remotivate managements and bring about substantial short-term improvements in profits more than it values businessmen who invest heavily and aim for growth in the long term. In the 1950s and 1960s the darlings of the City were men like Sir Charles Clore who built up Sears, the chain which owns Selfridges and most of the High Street shoe shops, and Sir Isaac Wolfson who created Great Universal Stores. In the 1970s it was Jim Slater, Sir Maxwell Joseph and their imitators who were given a virtual blank cheque to do what they liked with British industry. And in the 1980s industrialists such as Lord Hanson of Hanson Trust, Sir Owen Green of BTR, Sir Nigel Broackes of Trafalgar House, and Alec Monk of Dee Corporation are the favourites. They run some of the largest companies in Britain, but they have been built substantially by acquisition rather than internal growth.

Fund managers have come to favour companies which promise instant profits – whether or not these are the result of genuine organic growth as opposed to rationalisation after takeover bids. Companies they like are those which have shown consistent upward growth of earnings per share, and which make a lot of takeover bids. Their love affair with the conglomerate Hanson Trust is a case in point. It had a spectacular eleven-fold rise in its share price from 1980 to 1985.[22]

Companies which do not attract investment managers are those which embark on a ten-year strategy which does not immediately pay off, and which brings a short-term fall in profits. Thorn EMI came into this category after chairman Peter Laister's ambitious plans fell foul of poor timing[23] and he paid too much for some of his acquisitions. Profits fell; the non-executive directors then ousted him. If they had not, according to Sir Graham Wilkins, leader of the putsch, 'the institutions would have lost patience, and sold the company to the first bidder who came along'.[24] The effect of the Thorn experience went far beyond the fate of one chief executive, as the Governor of the Bank of England recognised:[25]

Industry tends to argue that the preoccupation of financial

investors with the short term makes it difficult for industry to spend as much as it knows it should on the development of new technology and of new products . . . . Boards are held back from action which they know is necessary.

The preoccupation with growth and takeovers led in some cases to unreasonable demands by fund managers for quick results from the industrial managers; or the managers thought it did, which amounted to the same thing from their point of view. In the 1980s the investing institutions, which, according to the Stock Exchange, control at least two-thirds of the nation's equity savings, were obsessed with the need for short-term profits. It became a regular complaint of the heads of British industry that they were in danger of being more concerned with appeasing the investors in the City than with taking long-term decisions for the good of their companies.[26]

A further criticism of the City was that it promoted takeovers simply to generate fees for itself, rather than to further industrial efficiency. According to the Director General of the British Institute of Management, Dr John Constable:[27]

Britain's merchant banks still have a powerful interest in maintaining merger and acquisition activities. For them activity means fees, and the prospect of fee income may well be a far stronger driving force than any aspect of industrial logic.

He also underlined the cultural problem caused by the City when he suggested further that:

the British and American societies see making money out of money a clever and more desirable activity than making money out of making goods sold in a competitive market place. The former involves speculation, the latter requires investment.

It also goes some way to explaining how the rules of the Takeover Panel, having been drafted by merchant bankers rather than by industrialists, strongly favoured the aggressor in any takeover bid – a bias some takeover specialists would concede.[28] This bias arises out of the strict timetable imposed on all bids by the Takeover Panel, which are allowed to run for no more than sixty days after the despatch of the first official document outlining the offer. The rules also stipulate that the shareholder must have two clear weeks in which to make his decision before the final closing date. What happens in effect, however, is that the attacker has the final word, because it has the right to consider whether or not to increase its offer once shareholders are in receipt of all the profit forecasts or similar financial information from the defending side. This allows the bidder a clear run in the closing stages of the campaign, when most people make up their minds, and accounts at least in part for the reason why less than one in ten of the companies bid for in 1985 managed to retain their independence.[29]

Britain is not alone in this problem. In the United States in the mid-1980s there was a serious debate on whether money managers were ruining the economy because of their obsession with short-term performance.[30] The argument was that fund managers bought shares and expected each quarter to show an improvement in profits. The moment there was a slow-down they sold the shares, and as the prices fell the company became vulnerable to a takeover. The management of companies therefore became totally preoccupied with short-term gains to satisfy restive shareholders. Research and development budgets were slashed. Projects which would pay off in five years time but which would harm profits in the meantime because of their start-up costs, were dismissed as too risky. The immediate closure of a plant which was losing money was preferred to long-term efforts to turn it round which might cause a drain on profits and dent the growth curve. And the cumulative effect of these measures was to bring about a serious reduction in the competitiveness of the economy – all of which went some way to explaining why the United States became so vulnerable to import penetration from Japan, a country where the emphasis was long-term and oriented towards medium-term market share rather than short-term profit.

Even the Bank of England became worried. Governor

Leigh-Pemberton noted that 'it is a recurrent source of
concern and complaint that investment time horizons are
unduly short in Britain, that they have been growing
shorter and that they are shorter there than they are in
other countries'.[31] His executive director for industrial
policy, David Walker, produced figures which confirmed
that major institutions were substantially less interested
than before in buying and holding shares for long-term
growth. He showed that the average life of a share in an
insurance company portfolio had dropped from nine years
in 1979 to just over five years in 1984, and the average life
of a unit trust investment in the same period from three
years to under two years.[32]

Walker demonstrated that the trend was partly due to
irreversible factors like the greater sophistication of
investment management techniques, the greater liquidity
of markets, the reduction of restrictions and controls on
where money could be invested, and the greater availability of financial instruments such as options which provided
alternative ways of participating in the stock markets
without holding shares. He warned that the trend was
likely to get worse once the London stock market was
deregulated. Earlier moves in New York had led to a major
increase in the turnover on that exchange; in the ten years
from 1974 to 1984 turnover rose from 20 per cent to 50 per
cent of the value of the shares quoted. The average
portfolio life of an American share was two years. In the
same decade the figure for portfolio life in London was 5.5
years.

The blame for the change in emphasis was laid squarely
at the door of the fund managers. They needed performance to achieve portfolio growth because this was how they
were judged and how they secured more fund management
contracts. If they failed to perform, then they lost those
contracts and went out of business. They therefore took
decisions which made short-term financial sense but made
nonsense of wider medium-term industrial strategy. They
admitted as much to the Governor of the Bank of England,
who quoted them as telling him:[33]

The managers of large pension funds tend to accept that they now give greater weight to short-term performance, but assert that this is because they find their own role judged by trustees on the basis of league tables of performance over very short time scales. They therefore feel obliged to tailor their investment strategies to match. As they put it, there is no point in buying a share in a three years time horizon if you are not going to be managing the portfolio next year.

The problem is that it is possible for fund managers to ruin the economy, as the Americans suspected. Short-term thinking eats into the industrial fabric and has undermined Britain's ability to compete. But the irony is that at this point it begins to act against the interests of the City to the extent that the City needs a flourishing viable industrial client base to ensure its future prosperity. This is a problem which other industrial countries – with the notable exception of the United States – do not have to confront, and it is one which arises directly out of the strength of the City relative to the power of the industrial base.

Curiously the City's love affair with takeover bids also flew in the face of the policy of the Conservative Government and its Chancellor of the Exchequer, Nigel Lawson. Though it refers very few bids to the Monopolies Commission, and then almost always on the grounds of restriction of competition, the Government is well aware that takeovers lead to the concentration of industrial power. The Conservative Government's policy has been to favour small units and it gives generous tax benefits through the Business Expansion Scheme to assist the development of such enterprises, the reasoning being that in the United States and Japan, the two most successful economies in the world, firms employing less than 500 people account for well over half of all private sector jobs, compared to well under half in the UK.[34]

What is most interesting about this clash between City and government and between City and industry is that the City did moderate its views. Once the concern was made apparent by the Governor of the Bank of England, the

mood changed. Within months it led to the defeat of takeover bids which previously would have succeeded. The
most notable of these was in January 1987 when BTR, the
acquisitive conglomerate, withdrew its hostile bid for
Pilkington, a traditional long-term investor in the glass
industry. Informal sounding of the institutions made it
clear that the City did not believe it could support the bid.

At the same time the City has gone out of its way to
foster the creation of smaller units as favoured by the
Government. It has helped to carve them from the
industrial giants which in earlier years it had helped to put
together – companies like Grand Metropolitan and Reed
International which had grown by acquisition in the early
1970s but had failed to shine. The City's solution in these
cases was to encourage the breaking up of these companies,
by providing finance for management buyouts.[35] Mecca
was spun off from Grand Metropolitan in 1986, and almost
the entire home products and building materials activities
of Reed were similarly sold off in a series of deals in the
mid-1980s. Significantly many of the companies being sold
off had been independent before, but had been taken over
in the previous round of takeover frenzy some fifteen years
earlier.

Thus in several phases over the last thirty years the City
has first supported takeovers and then had to put up the
capital to have them unwound. The ensuing massive
shuffling of industrial assets has led to equally massive
profits for the City, the fund managers, the brokers, and
the advisers, but with no conspicuous increase in the
efficiency of the companies concerned, or of the economy. It
is hard to resist the conclusion that the whole exercise did
little to enhance Britain's industrial performance – and as
a result did little to enhance the long-term returns of those
same City fund managers who have been obliged to invest
in British industry.

Investment Protection Committees

If such shuffling were to be avoided in future, the Bank of
England realised that it needed to change the attitudes of

the City fund managers. But there was no sign that this could be achieved. The organisation of saving in Britain has given great power to two groups – the building societies and the fund managers. Building societies have traditionally been confined to property and investment in government securities, and in spite of liberalisation in the 1980s, are not part of the argument here. It is the investment fund managers who have too often failed to take the responsibility that came with their power.

The former head of fund management group M and G, David Hopkinson, criticised his colleagues for not bringing Guinness chief executive Ernest Saunders to heel when he reneged on promises to appoint an independent chairman to his board, and accused them of failing to act because they did not want a public row which would do short-term damage to the value of their investment.[36] David Walker of the Bank of England was reduced to talking longingly of the 'benefit which would accrue' if institutional shareholders were 'more ready to press on companies their concerns to see improved performance'.[37] He argued that shareholders should agitate to ensure that companies were well managed and that competent boards of directors were in place. Sir Francis Tombs, Chairman of Turner and Newall and of Rolls Royce, claims that in his experience institutions are so indifferent to the conduct of a company's affairs, that they rarely even fill in their proxy voting cards for the election of directors.[38]

The insurance, pension and similar investing institutions grow increasingly powerful. With a never-ending supply of new cash pouring in from the contributions of occupational pension schemes, insurance premiums and the dividends on their existing portfolios, the amount of share capital in their hands increases daily. And with every new share they buy their power increases. Major shareholders like the Prudential, or the Coal Board pension fund, regularly have shareholdings of 5, 10 or 15 per cent in companies. Individually their holdings are large enough to embarrass management. If they were to act together, there is hardly a company in the land, short of those few still under family control, where they could not vote out a board of directors of which they disapproved and vote in a new one.

But the City in the past has almost always ducked this challenge. The fund managers have believed their job was to invest money and that they should leave the managers alone to manage. They argued that they knew nothing about running companies; nor did they want to learn. If a company failed to perform, then the accepted solution was to sell the shares.

Nor, on the occasions when they have moved in the past, has the policy been well thought out. In 1982, Sir Robert Clark, chairman of Hill Samuel and also a non-executive director of UDS, a large department store chain, received a telephone call from a senior investment manager of the Prudential. He was asked to inform Sir Bernard Lyons, then chairman of UDS, that if there was not a new chairman nominated at the next annual meeting of the company four months hence, the Prudential would vote its shares in full public view at the meeting against Lyons' re-appointment.[39] Though he could certainly have mustered more votes than the Prudential, the public humiliation would have destroyed Lyons' credibility; he therefore stepped down in favour of Sir Robert himself, there being no other candidate. But barely had he been voted into office when a bid came from Hanson Trust. The Prudential, though it had secured the board change it wanted, nevertheless accepted the bid.

This attitude is currently being re-thought to a limited degree – for one simple reason. As the investing institutions have got larger, their shareholdings have got bigger, and they have found they cannot quietly sell out without precipitating a major slide in the share price of the company concerned, thereby alerting other holders to the problems and causing a possible collapse of confidence. They are now locked into the holdings they have bought, and therefore, if they want a company's performance to improve, they have to do something about it.

Merchant banks, too, are reluctantly accepting that they have to force management changes on their clients, even though it is a thankless task, which brings down on them the wrath of the deposed, while not necessarily securing the trust and confidence of the newcomers. Nevertheless, a bank like Hill Samuel, with roughly 600 company clients in the small- to medium-sized range, estimates that it secures on average 10 management changes a year, ranging from a clean sweep in the boardroom to the more common and discreet appointment of a new chief executive or finance director.[40] According to David Hopkinson, however, progress in persuading people to turn a company round rather than sell at the first sign of trouble has been greatly hampered by the fear of doing damage to short-term performance. He maintains that this is why the institutions acquiesced in the denial of the Guinness chairmanship to Sir Thomas Risk in spite of previous promises from chief executive Ernest Saunders.[41]

As we saw in an earlier chapter, in the absence of merchant bank involvement, the solution has been to form investment protection committees to deal with specific problems as they occur, and to thrash out a co-ordinated response to them. These are effective in preparing position papers on the correct response to takeover bids and in forming a view on the price of large new issues. When a committee decides it does not like a takeover bid, it will make discreet but strenuous attempts to have the policy changed. This pressure is exerted by inviting the chairman of the company making the bid, with or without his advisers, to a meeting, where he is told quite bluntly that his policy will not be supported and that he institutions will not give him any financial backing if he persists.

Generally speaking, however, the institutional investor is not concerned with the subtlety of long-term effects or the wider implications of a takeover, or even if it is in the interests of the company making the bid. The matter is considered instead solely from the point of view of the target company, and according to Legal and General's General Manager (Investment) P. W. Simon:[42]

> unless there are special features which make the case non-standard, the institution's decision will be based quite simply on its assessment of the price being offered as well as

its assessment of what would happen to the share price of the
target company if the bid failed.

The visibility of the pressure varies, however. When
newspaper and magazine publisher Fleet Holdings attempted to take over Aitken Hume, a financial services group,
in the spring of 1985, Fleet's institutional investors
disapproved because it was such a different business,
though no one made any public comment. They simply
informed Fleet's merchant bank advisers, who relayed
their unhappiness to the Fleet board and the deal was
quietly dropped. The previous autumn they had been much
more overt. The rescue of Johnson Matthey Bankers
involved an issue of shares in the parent company to the
banks participating in the rescue, at a substantial discount
on the market price. The institutions who were not a party
to this deal retained a merchant banker, John Nelson of
Kleinwort Benson, to negotiate to have the original deal
unscrambled, and to ensure that the institutions and other
outside shareholders were given an opportunity to take
part in the rescue and to obtain an equal share of the
favourable terms. Without this action they would have
been shut out and stood to see their percentage stakes in
the company substantially diluted.

Similarly, as we have seen in Chapter 3, in January
1987 the insurance IPC moved decisively to veto a
proposed share option scheme for the senior executives of
Burton Group, which they considered over-generous. The
proposals were substantially scaled down after their
publication, but before they were voted on by shareholders.

Again it is worth repeating that when the institutions
say they want a board strengthened, boards do change. Sir
Francis Tombs was brought in to revitalise Turner and
Newall, Sir Michael Edwardes to sort out Dunlop, Sir John
Cuckney to salvage John Brown. Rumblings of discontent
conveyed to the non-executive directors of Thorn, Beecham
and STC over lunch in City stockbroking offices led to
boardroom revolts in all those companies and the abrupt
departure of their chief executives, Peter Laister, Ronald
Halstead and Sir Kenneth Corfield. If these hints are

ignored by the board, then the institutions let it be known that they would welcome a takeover bid. Sooner or later a merchant bank or industrialist takes the hint and one is launched which the institutions then promptly support, and secure their management changes that way. For example, the small Electrical Services Supply company was taken over in a £30 million deal in March 1985 because the institutions, having run out of patience with the management, approached Hambros Bank and asked it to organise a takeover. Three years before the British arm of Woolworth was taken over by a consortium formed specially for the purpose of the bid, and organised by Victor Blank at Charterhouse.

There are weaknesses in the system, however. The investment protection committees are much better at dealing with short-term issues like takeovers than with long-term struggles to get one chief executive replaced by another. Co-ordinating a campaign to get rid of a chief executive takes a great deal of time, and unless the performance has been poor for very many years most fund managers are not prepared to take on the extra duties involved in such a task. In most cases therefore managements are left to their own devices and do not find the institutions put pressure on them, in spite of urgings from the Governor of the Bank of England that they have a duty 'to positively promote industrial development and change'.[43]

9

Is the City
Good for Britain?

The case in favour of the City has two prongs. First, the City is of great importance to the country as a source of employment and invisible earnings; because of its contribution to the balance of payments it makes a material difference to the whole nation's prosperity, not simply to those who work within the Square Mile. Second, in a democratic country people have a perfect right to do what they like within the law. The people and institutions within the City are doing no more than exercising that right, and should continue to be allowed to do so.

The case against the City is multifaceted. First, there is the argument that the City does not create the kind of society that should exist in a healthy democracy. It inveighs against the City as a symbol of privilege, a close-knit community geared to the preservation of wealth for a select few.

Second, there is the argument that the City takes more than its fair share of the nation's intellectual resources, as measured by the chosen career paths of the top graduates from the best universities. It inveighs against the City as a magnet, which draws the most talented of the population, at the expense of manufacturing industry, because of its ability to pay far higher salaries.

Third, there is the argument that the City is too powerful within the framework of the British economy, and that City institutions act out of self-interest in ways which are not necessarily good for the country as a whole. And fourth it is alleged that the fund managers of the City starve British industry of capital because of their enthusiasm for investing abroad.

What the City earns

Financial services are vitally important to the UK economy in terms of employment and gross national product. In the mid-1980s some 1.89 million people were employed in the industry, and it contributed some £37 billion to gross national product.

And financial services are becoming ever more important in modern Britain. In the decade from the mid-1970s to the mid-1980s the proportion of the total workforce employed in the financial services sector rose from 6 to 10 per cent. At the same time, an ever increasing share of total national income was generated by financial services, which rose from 11.42 per cent to 13.21 per cent in the five years to 1985.[1] From this it can be seen that the financial services sector is among the most productive in the economy; 10 per cent of the workforce generate 13.2 per cent of the wealth of the nation.

We saw in Table 4.2 how the overseas earnings of the financial sector have grown from £2 billion ('000 million) in 1980 to £7.5 billion in 1985, of which banking accounts for £2.1 billion, insurance companies for £1.4 billion, and the Lloyd's of London insurance market for £1.2 billion. The securities industry as a whole earns profits, but these are small in comparison, and the Stock Exchange brought in just £106 million against £43 million in 1980.

So while the City as a whole is undoubtedly a great national asset, the Stock Exchange and securities industry, the area of the City which looms highest in the national consciousness and which has potentially the greatest impact on the domestic economy, is not a significant earner of foreign exchange. It may become one, if the changes set in train by Big Bang successfully establish London as the global centre for international trading in equities, but that goal has still to be achieved. The City's reputation as a money-spinner rides on the back of the insurance and banking industries, two areas, notwithstanding the frauds at Lloyd's of London, which generally arouse less controversy.

How other countries compare.   There is no doubt that the City's surplus on invisibles helps to restore the international economic balance. Without it Germany and Japan would be vastly more powerful than they are, as is shown in the figures in Table 9.1 which demonstrate how the British economy has a larger income from invisibles than any other country in the world with the exception of the United States. They further demonstrate how this surplus compares with huge deficits in Germany, Japan, Brazil and Canada.

Table 9.1 World invisibles 1984 (US $m.)

Country	Net invisible receipts
Top five	
USA	33,483
United Kingdom	11,234
Switzerland	6,864
France	6,844
Spain	5,632
Bottom five	
Brazil	−9,952
Japan	−12,949
West Germany	−13,217
Saudi Arabia	−13,713
Canada	−15,019

Source: Committee on Invisible Exports

These figures include all invisibles, and therefore show the contribution of tourism, transport and other non-financial services. The comparison with other countries is hampered because they do not use the same basis for calculating the contribution of their financial sector. But in the British case it is approximately two-thirds of the net surplus.[2]

Overseas investment

The City controls where the bulk of British private sector savings are invested, whether in industry or services, at home or overseas. Table 9.2 shows how much it directed abroad, broken down into direct and portfolio investment and the special-case oil sector, and how the total grew in the ten years to 1984 – a period which encompasses five years before and five years after the abolition of exchange controls in 1979.

Table 9.2 UK private investment overseas (£m.)

Year	Direct	Portfolio	Oil	Total
1975	1,171	59	137	1,367
1976	2,145	−90	214	2,269
1977	1,885	−12	461	2,334
1978	2,710	1,073	821	4,604
1979	3,035	909	2,858	6,808
1980	3,391	3,150	1,566	8,107
1981	4,671	4,090	1,418	10,179
1982	2,246	6,200	1,982	10,428
1983	3,199	6,110	1,932	11,241
1984	1,894	8,810	3,881	14,585

Note: Negative sign means dis-investment.
Source: Central Statistical Office, *UK Balance of Payments*, 1985 edition.

The figures reveal that there was a considerable amount of overseas investment before the abolition of exchange controls, when it was still necessary to obtain prior permission from the Bank of England. But the figures for portfolio investment surged dramatically after 1979 when the res-

traints were removed, while those for industrial investment overseas showed a much more modest rate of increase
and a sharp decline in 1984. The period did coincide,
however, with a marked recession at home and a cash
squeeze on industry which constrained its freedom to invest anywhere, coupled with a major inflow into the City of
earnings generated from North Sea oil. To put the figures
further in perspective, the 1983 total of £11,241 million
compared with a Public Sector Borrowing Requirement
that year of £11,557 million and fixed domestic investment
expenditure by manufacturing industry of £5,666 million.[3]

Table 9.3 demonstrates that British pension fund investment managers are much more inclined to invest overseas
than are their counterparts in other countries. The case
against the City's activity in this area is argued succinctly
by the TUC,[4] which says that since 1979 there has been a
massive increase in overseas investment. Its research suggests that the value of overseas portfolio investment rose to
£69 billion by 1985, while the level of overseas assets in
pension fund portfolios trebled to around 18 per cent between 1979 and 1985.

The fact that pension fund holdings of foreign assets rose
so fast reflects, at least in part, the pent-up demand from

*Table 9.3 Foreign investment as a percentage of private
sector pension assets*

Country	1980	1985	1990 (est.)
USA	1	3	8
Britain	9	18	25
Japan	1	8	20
Netherlands	4	9	15
Canada	7	8	10
Switzerland	4	4	8
Germany	2	3	6
Australia	0	5	12

Estimates by Intersec. Research Corporation.
Source: *Global Investor Relations Report*, an occasional paper published
Gavin Anderson Inc., February 1987.

the period before 1979 when foreign investment was difficult. There has been a once-and-for-all correction. Since
then the figures tend to fluctuate dramatically from quarter to quarter, and between institutions, some building up
foreign holdings, while others are running them down. But
the experience of the first quarter of 1986 was perhaps
typical. In that period some £10.2 billion flowed into the
financial sector, of which £8.5 billion went to the financial
institutions; of this some £2.9 billion went abroad, £1.8
billion into equities, and £1.1 billion into foreign corporate
fixed interest securities.[5]

In his 1987 budget speech the Chancellor of the Exchequer reported that British portfolio investment overseas
was in excess of £100 billion, more pro rata than any other
country with the exception of Japan, and he claimed that
in the years to come the earnings on this investment would
provide a major source of wealth for Britain.[6] Table 9.4
shows that this claim is justified, for it illustrates that
earnings from abroad were already high enough in the
early 1980s to offset the ever greater sums going overseas.
Indeed, the 1984 earnings generated by investment abroad
were greater than the total overseas outflow year by year
prior to 1983. Nor was the separate allegation that British

*Table 9.4 Effect on balance of payments of UK private
overseas investment 1979–84 (£m.)*

	1979	1980	1981	1982	1983	1984
1. Total overseas investment	−6,802	−8,107	−10,179	−10,428	−11,241	−14,585
2. Earnings on direct investment	2,483	2,934	3,456	3,084	4,051	4,128
3. Earnings on portfolio inv.	540	750	990	1,630	2,590	3,520
4. Earnings on oil company inv.	2,981	2,113	1,870	1,835	2,188	3,033
5. Balance of inv. minus earnings	−438	−2,310	−3,773	−3,879	−2,412	−3,904

Source: David Shepherd, 'Assessing the Consequences of Overseas Investment',
Royal Bank of Scotland Review, January 1987, figures derived from Central Statistical Office, *UK Balance of Payments 1985*.

industry was being starved of investment funds as a result of increasing tranches of foreign investment supported by these facts. Overseas investment may not yet be approaching the point at which it is self-funding, but the net outflow of £3.9 billion in 1984 was well under 5 per cent of Gross National Product.

An analysis produced by the Treasury in March 1985[7] which covers broadly the same period as Table 9.4 showed that in 1979 Britain's net assets overseas were a bare £12.5 billion, equivalent to 6.5 per cent of national income. Five years later at the end of 1984 they were £70 billion, equivalent to 22 per cent of national income, a five-fold increase in five years. This increase is roughly equivalent to the £54 billion contribution made by North Sea oil to the British economy in the same period.

This is the basis for the allegation that the City shipped the benefits of North Sea oil abroad to employ other nations' workforces, while depriving British manufacturing of its investment lifeblood. As the TUC put it, such an overseas investment policy would result in less not more industrial capacity in the UK and fewer not more jobs:[8]

The City's investment policies eventually become self fulfilling as they lock the UK economy into a vicious cycle of decline. Putting funds into UK industry becomes less and less attractive and the investment gap between the UK and its leading competitors grows ever wider.

The City has two answers to this. First, that the current level of investment abroad is insignificant by historical standards. By the middle of the nineteenth century, overseas assets were the equivalent of some 40 per cent of national income and by the eve of the First World War they had risen to a massive 180 per cent of national income. It was the ability to sell these assets in huge quantities that enabled the government of the day to meet its wartime debts. The City argues that by pouring Britain's oil wealth overseas in the 1980s it has been saving a profligate nation from itself, and creating assets for which it will be duly grateful when the oil revenues run out in the next century.

Second, that the investment earns a better return overseas, and that the City would be failing in its duty if it did not take advantage of this. Indeed, it might be acting against the law if it did not do so. In 1984 the principle that the City should invest its money where the funds, rather than the country, obtained the best returns was upheld by the courts. The National Union of Mineworkers, in its role as one of the trustees of its pension fund, tried to prevent the fund managers investing money overseas, seeking instead to have the cash poured into creating new factories and employment in Britain. It also wanted a ban on investment in the shares of companies involved with competing fuels like oil. But Mr Justice Megarry ruled in the High Court that the fund managers' duty was to seek the best return for their members' funds; he saw no obligation for the managers to use the money in ways which might or might not assist the continuation of the coal industry.

It should also be noted that the figures for total overseas assets exaggerate the real outflow, because a substantial part of the increase in assets is the result of capital gains. Of the £57.5 billion increase cited by the Treasury, only £18 billion represented net new investment; the remaining two-thirds represent the increase in the sterling value of those overseas assets, and are therefore a capital gain.

If current values are maintained then, as Chancellor Nigel Lawson suggested, the implications for Britain's economy are legion. If the 1987 overseas portfolio were to yield a 10 per cent return, it would generate £10 billion, which would be the equivalent of 2.5 times the Public Sector Borrowing Requirement that year, or of the bulk of the deficit on trade in manufactured goods, or the tax revenue from North Sea oil. In fact, the income is much less, of the order of £5 billion, reflecting the fact that the portfolio is still immature and is heavily biased towards equity investment rather than fixed interest securities. But it is, even at that level, a major contributor to the economy. And as the purpose of equity investment is to secure future growth, then the income from the portfolio must be expected to rise substantially in the future. It may well be that in the 1990s as the oil runs out the country will indeed have reason to be grateful for the City's overseas investment of the 1980s.

Preservation of privilege

A major criticism of the City is directed at its role in preserving the divisions of wealth and status, and the class structure. The fortunes created in the last century are in many cases the foundations of wealth and power today. The Barings, for example, are an extended family of enormous wealth and influence which goes far beyond an ability to make money. One of the family, Lord Cromer, took time off in the last century to run Egypt more or less like a country estate, while the present holder of the title has been Ambassador to the United States and Governor of the Bank of England. Another member, Thomas, the first Lord Northbrooke, was First Lord of the Admiralty and Viceroy of India. And a third, Sir Evelyn Baring, son of the first Lord Cromer, was created Lord Howick for his contribution to the development of Kenya, Rhodesia and elsewhere.[9]

The current head of the family bank, Sir John Baring, is heir to the sixth Baron Ashburton, the family having no less than five separate peerages – Ashburton, Howick, Cromer, Northbrooke and Revelstoke – a number not achieved by any family since the Wars of the Roses. Sir John is a trustee of the Rhodes Trust and the National Gallery, a fellow of Eton College and an Honorary Fellow of Hertford College, Oxford. Like his father, he holds the title of Receiver General to the Duchy of Cornwall. He is also a member of the Board of Governors of the Bank of England, a director of BP and, until late 1984, of Dunlop, Chairman of the Outwich Investment Trust and of the NEDC committee on Finance for Industry, and a member of the General Council of the British Bankers Association, as well as being a former chairman of the Accepting Houses Committee, the trade association of the most influential of the city's merchant banks. Other previous interests include being a member of the British Transport Docks board from 1966 to 1971, a director of Royal Insurance from 1964 to 1982, a member of the Council for the Securities Industry from 1977 to 1981 and a member of the

President's Committee of the Confederation of British Industry from 1976 to 1979.

What the Barings have achieved is perhaps the most spectacular, but is certainly not untypical, of the experience of a range of City families. These are familes whose wealth is enhanced by membership of Lloyd's, with the huge tax benefits that brings,[10] and passed down comfortably through the generations by judicious and timely use of family trusts, and whose children have always been able to find secure employment through their family connections in banking, broking or insurance. As such, their wealth has proved enduring and their influence, as the Baring connection shows, spreads right through the fabric of society.

The existence in the City of a large number of people who are there because of inherited wealth has contributed to the 'them and us' feeling so fiercely exploited by British politicians and labour leaders, which has been one cause of British industrial unrest. It has also been a reason why the City has been distanced from the country as a whole, and why, in spite of the nation having the third largest stock exchange in the world, there was until the privatisation programme of the 1980s widespread ignorance of the possibilities of share ownership. This, in turn, created a lack of identification with, and belief in, capitalism, which again served to undermine the economy.

The changes of the 1980s, however, have undermined the validity of the old criticism of the City as a haven for the elite. The 450 foreign banks operating in London have no truck with the old school tie and hire and fire staff on merit. The British banks have had to respond in kind to stay competitive. The new markets put the emphasis on intellectual skills, flexibility and the ability to take controlled risks in areas such as market-making and the issuing of securities much more than on family connections. The securities houses hire people with the required intellectual abilities where they can find them, regardless of whether they come from City families.

Most of all, the expansion in demand for financial services and the huge increase in employment in the City has led to an influx of people from non-City backgrounds. 'Big Bang was the signal for the cloth cap brigades to take over', says Dr Paul Neild, a director of Phillips and Drew.[11] His confident view was based on the perception that Big Bang would concentrate Stock Exchange business into fewer hands, and put a premium on those firms which could offer clients comprehensive skills including research and the ability to conduct business in huge volumes of shares – a service which necessarily exposes the securities house to major risk as it has to hold the shares on its own account while re-selling them to clients. These risk-management skills owe least to the old boy network. A Stock Exchange survey in Spring 1987 showed that 50 per cent of turnover is now concentrated in 10 firms. In transactions of over £250,000 or more, representing 50 per cent of turnover, five firms account for half the business.[12]

Table 9.5 demonstrates how in 1987 Neild was beginning to be proved correct. A survey of 115 fund managers, with collective investments worth £100 billion, was conducted by the opinion pollsters MORI, and published in *The Sunday Times*. It showed which brokers were the first choice among leading fund managers, and which, though not first, still got more than 10 per cent of their business.

Table 9.5 London's most successful brokers

Broker	First choice of fund managers	More than 10% of business
James Capel	26	24
Phillips & Drew	10	31
Scrimgeour Vickers	9	32
Hoare Govett	11	29
Rowe & Pitman Mullens	7	27
Wood Mackenzie	13	18
Cazenove	6	18

Source: *The Sunday Times*, 15 February 1987.

The top four firms are no longer British-owned and therefore cannot be considered part of the traditional City establishment. Hongkong and Shanghai Bank owns James Capel, Union Bank of Switzerland Phillips and Drew, Citicorp, the American banking group, owns Scrimgeour Vickers, and another American bank, Security Pacific, owns Hoare Govett. The best placed British-owned firm was Rowe and Pitman, part of the Warburg empire, followed by Wood Mackenzie, which is owned by Hill Samuel. Cazenove, which has remained independent, is perhaps the one firm which represents the traditional Stock Exchange way of doing business – through contacts and connections. But by 1987 it was slipping down the list, and as it slipped it symbolised the diminishing importance of the old guard and the rising professionalism of the City's new elite.

Salaries and the City

Table 9.6 shows that the salaries of the top executives in Britain's leading companies increased dramatically in the six years after the Conservative Government cut the top rates of marginal tax to 60 per cent, and made it worthwhile to reward executives with salary increases rather than tax-free perks. Nevertheless, the salaries paid by industry are poor in comparison with what is available in

Table 9.6 The pay of top UK industrialists (£)

	1979–80	*1985–86*
Grand Metropolitan	50,380	176,289
Marks & Spencer	64,077	217,016
Tesco	42,407	118,416
Imperial	68,000	171,368
ICI	124,380	312,991
BAT	94,726	226,830
GEC	75,000	177,000
RTZ	66,000	145,993
BP	120,385	260,972
Courtaulds	65,620	126,288
GKN	82,342	145,000
Rover Group	57,200	98,367

Source: Company annual reports.

the City. The public flotation prospectus of Mercury Asset Management, for example, revealed that the executive directors of that company earned an average of £150,000 each including bonus in the six months to September 1986, and in the absence of further bonuses would earn an average of £350,000 for the year.

This underlines the discrepancy in salary levels. First, Mercury Asset Management is a tiny company, with 481 employees including the directors; it made profits of less than £20 million. ICI, BAT and several of the others in Table 9.6 have 100,000 or more employees, and made profits in 1986 of £1 billion.

Second, the top people in industry spend much of their lives getting to their positions, which they generally do not attain until they have turned 50. They are then normally at their peak earning power for only a few years before retirement. The directors in the City, on the other hand, are big earners at a much earlier age. In Mercury Asset Management's case a majority were under 40, and they can expect to maintain their earning power much longer.

Third, the high salaries in the City are spread around much more widely. In industry no one in the companies listed came close to matching the salary of the chief executive. Indeed, most industrial companies can muster no more than one person earning £100,000 a year, and you are considered to be doing well if you are earning £40,000 by the time you are 40. In the City, everyone in a position of responsibility earns a huge salary. There is thus much more opportunity for the young graduate to make much more money, much more quickly, and generally in much more congenial surroundings than he (or she – one MAM director is a 38-year-old woman) would have in industry.

The size of the organisation is not the only guide to payment scales, of course, and defenders of City salaries lay great stress on the fact that the big earners have responsibility for hundreds of millions of pounds and can in a matter of minutes, by a single misjudgement, make or lose their firms far more than they earn. They also stress the penalties for failure. When they are succesful they earn well; but there is now a much lower tolerance of failure or mediocrity than in industry.

In addition, high salaries are available at much lower levels too, with equity analysts in their twenties earning £100,000, and equity and bond salesmen of similar age in charge of small teams on profit-sharing arrangements making in excess of £200,000. The prospects for further advancement are also significantly greater than in industry. Though Sir Ralph Halpern of the Burton Group became the first British industrialist to earn more than £1 million thanks to a successful profit-linked bonus scheme, such salaries are commonplace in the City, and most of the big banks or broking houses, and particularly the American organisations based in London, would employ people whose salary would approach that level in a good year.

The result is that the City took the pick of the talent from the universities, or at one remove from the professions of accountancy and law, once it started recruiting seriously in the 1970s, and industry found itself starved of talent. David Hardy, Chairman of Globe, the largest investment trust, but also of Swan Hunter the shipbuilders, who has had a distinguished career in both fields, insists that for years the City had told industry to pay more, but without effect. So the City continued to attract the best talent, which, now that it has been liberated by deregulation and the opportunities for innovation and new business brought about by the change in the markets, 'is really starting to perform'.[13]

Against such a background industry cannot compete, nor will it be able to do so as long as the financial services industry booms, and sees the need to match the salaries available in the United States and other financial centres. It may not be the City's fault that there is such a disparity in the rate of return for the effort expended, but it can scarcely be good for the country.

The City and industry

The hardest case for the City to answer concerns its relationships with industry – whether it provides sufficient capital for British industry, and whether its emphasis on

short-term results means that it does not provide the climate of security which industry needs if it is to plan ahead.
The case against the City is not confined to left-wing politicians and the TUC. We saw in an earlier chapter that
Conservative Minister Nicholas Edwards accused the City
in 1986 of being myopic. That same year a fringe meeting
at the National Young Conservatives annual conference
heard British industrialist Gordon Gaddes, President of
the trade association BEAMA, appeal for greater co-operation, understanding and long-term investment in industry
by the banks and the Stock Exchange:[14]

> Serious consideration should be given by Government to the
> devastating effects that large and short term fluctuations in
> the various markets – the foreign exchange, the Stock Ex-
> change and the money markets – can have on business
> enterprise, dependent as it is on long lead times in both
> planning and recouping investment . . . . British industry
> looks wistfully at Germany and Japan where co-operation
> with banks in the form of share owning is one of the keys to
> industrial success.

One complaint is that the City is prejudiced against
investment in Britain because it feels estranged, and of a
different cultural background, from the people of the de-
pressed industrial heartlands. This is an attitude summed
up by the banker who, when asked why there was so little
private investment in impoverished parts of Britain, said,
in a reference to a well publicised occasion in 1981 when
the Minister for the Environment took leading City figures
to see for themselves conditions in one of Britain's most
deprived inner cities:[15]

> Politicians hire buses and take businessmen round
> Merseyside. Well, would you invest there? In a lot of bloody-
> minded Liverpudlians? People complain that the City does
> not invest in places like Liverpool. Why should it? It isn't
> efficient.

A second complaint is that the City is risk-averse. The
argument is that the original role of the investment manager was to invest the fortunes of the City's wealthy families. The emphasis of such portfolio management was on

the preservation of wealth, and many portfolios were structured as investment trusts with clear restrictions on the
investment policy they could pursue. Indeed, Henderson
Administration, which is still among the best established
of Britain's investment management groups, was founded
by Alexander Henderson, first Lord Faringdon, precisely
because he did not trust his son's judgement, and wanted to
ensure that the family fortune he had made passed intact
to his grandchildren.[16] Such a move was not untypical.
Following the entrepreneurial spurt of the Victorian era,
the City investment managers were trained to be cautious,
so creating a tradition of safe investment and secure yields
which has stayed with them even when, as now, the funds
they manage come from the general public through con-
tractual savings plans rather than from private portfolios.
As a consequence, investment managers are reluctant to
put money into an untried industrial project when they can
be sure of a guaranteed, though more modest, return from
a government security.

Pension and insurance company fund managers in Britain in 1985 held two-thirds of the equities on the Stock
Exchange, compared to only 20 per cent of the shares in
Tokyo held by similar Japanese institutions.[17] In addition,
the £200 billion of pension fund moneys are concentrated
in relatively few hands. Although there are 90,000 pension
schemes in the UK, 70,000 have fewer than 100 members.
Twenty-seven funds have assets of over £1 billion and the
five largest, the National Coal Board, British Telecom,
Electricity Supply, the Post Office and British Airways
between them account for more than £25 billion.[18] Aversion to risk on their part, therefore, coupled with the relatively greater financial power of fund managers in Britain compared to overseas, could indeed be a factor in the
country's poor investment record.

The fact remains that for a variety of reasons – the
relative attractiveness of foreign markets, the cultural
antipathy between the country's financial centre and its
industrial heartland, the relative lack of good industrial
management, and the shortage of well presented business
ideas – Britain had not throughout the 1970s and up to the

mid-1980s produced a sufficient number of new businesses
to revitalise the economy.

Takeovers. Critics argue that the City not only fails to
foster new businesses, but is also irresponsible in the way
it treats those which are established. Professional fund
managers have shorter time horizons and much less loyalty to company managements than individual shareholders
or owner managers. The effect of economic power being
concentrated in the hands of fund managers whose primary objective is investment performance is therefore to
shift the financial system away from investment and into
speculation.

One consequence of this is that elements in the City
foster the belief that it is more clever and desirable to
make money out of investing money, than to make money
out of making and selling goods in a competitive market
place. A second is that the City is keen to support takeover
bids, with one industrial company swallowing up another
regardless of whether the bid makes industrial sense.
From the fund manager's perspective, a takeover produces
an immediate gain in the value of his portfolio, and from
the perspective of the merchant banking community, it is a
source of massive fee income. This motivation may well
override industrial logic in prompting a merchant bank to
persuade a client to make a bid.

There have also been some in the City who raised their
voices against the takeover trend. David Tucker, one of the
senior investment managers with M and G, the leading
unit trust group, looked at the time and expense of takeover battles and commented that shareholders should question 'whether these displays of corporate machismo would
have been better directed to the care and improvement of
existing businesses'. He warned of an anti-City social and
political backlash, because he felt that takeovers
weakened the loyalty of shareholders towards the companies in which they invest. The consequence could well be
that they would not support industry through the next
recession, nor provide investment capital when it was
needed.[19]

Investors would again be perceived to have failed the interests of the community and Government would doubtless feel it necessary to interfere and direct investment to what it regards as the appropriate areas.

The danger inherent in a financial sector motivated only by the pursuit of profit was vividly brought home by the Guinness affair of 1987, when a Department of Trade and Industry investigation into the takeover of Distillers by Guinness the previous year found that, to ensure a Guinness success, the company had engaged in a massive exercise of artificially inflating its share price. A stream of resignations followed both from the company and from City firms like Morgan Grenfell which had played a major part in advising Guinness. Almost all the big takeover bids of the 1980s involved some massaging upwards of the bidder's share price, coupled with attacks designed to weaken the share prices of rival bidders, and of the target company. Indeed, these were considered an integral part of the takeover game. The lesson of the Guinness scandal has therefore been that the country cannot afford to allow major industrial issues to be settled in the financial market place, when it cannot trust the City not to rig that market place artificially.

The takeover activity of the 1980s has probably seriously damaged the economy. Such studies as have been done suggest that more than half the companies involved in takeover bids subsequently under-performed over the next ten years. Though takeover bids, and the accounting tricks which accompany them, frequently produce the illusion of growth in earnings per share, this is in many cases simply an illusion.[20] There therefore remains a major doubt about the City's judgement, given its willingness to support takeover activity, its lack of judgement in assessing bids, and its inability to see the medium-term consequences of its obsessive interest in short-term performance.

The challenge to the City

It is a mystery to people working in the City that the benefit which a prosperous financial services sector brings

to the country is not instantly appreciated and understood.
But this lack of appreciation stems from a failure of communication for which the City must assume a major responsibility. Now, having modernised its markets, the City
faces a series of challenges, and its success in meeting
them will determine whether it continues to prosper, or
whether it simply survives as a prelude to inexorable decline. The matter for regret is that because its communication has been so poor, it will have to fight these battles
without political or popular support.

Regulation.   First, the City faces a regulatory challenge.
It has prospered over the years by allowing and indeed
encouraging activities which would be illegal in certain
other countries. In the United States and Japan the banking industry and the securities industry are strictly sepa-
rated. A firm has to choose to be in one or the other; it
cannot be in both. It is therefore illegal for American or
Japanese commercial banks to operate also in their domestic securities markets. Until the 1980s this prohibition
mattered little, but it gradually became a major impedi-
ment to the commercial banks, because the lending of
money, which is the essence of traditional banking, was
giving way across the world to the securitisation of debt. In
other words, companies raised money by selling shares or
bonds direct to the public, rather than by raising bank
loans, but because the banks could not operate in the
securities business, they had to stand on the sidelines and
watch their customer base dwindle away.

What made London so important to American and
Japanese banks confronted with this dilemma was that
there was no such prohibition there and banks were free to
enter the securities business. And, communications being
good, from London they could reach to almost every market
in the world other than their original home base, where of
course the prohibition still stood. That is why so many
firms rushed to buy London stockbroking firms in the early
1980s, and it remains an important reason why the City is
a major international centre. Foreign firms can operate in
the City in ways which would be illegal if they attempted

them back home.

The whole ethos of the Eurodollar market – for twenty years the major engine of the City's growth – has been rooted in this culture. The practitioners in the market have been supervised to a greater or lesser degree by the Bank of England but the rein has always been loose, largely because Eurobonds were rarely sold to domestic British investors. The market therefore had no domestic political impact as the public were unaware of it, and no economic impact as companies did not use it.

The same culture was prevalent in the regulation of Lloyd's and the Stock Exchange. But as the deregulation of the 1980s gathered pace, it led to excesses in these markets, and to abuses of positions of trust which occurred on such a scale that they threatened the reputation of the City as a clean place in which to do business. The subsequent efforts to tighten up the rules centred on the passing of the Financial Services Act and the creation of a near statutory body, the Securities and Investments Board (SIB), which was for the first time to bring the force of law to the self-regulatory world of the City.

The weakness of the City in the past had not been absence of rules, however, albeit that the rules were non-statutory. It had been a lack of will on the part of the City fathers, particularly the Stock Exchange, to enforce those rules when they involved challenging the mighty and long established names in the City. Until the mid-1980s their efforts to catch insider dealers were described by some with first-hand experience as inept, half-hearted and lacking in serious commitment.[21] But the SIB cannot hope to operate successfully without the full co-operation of those in the markets whom it seeks to regulate, and it remains to be seen whether those of the establishment who are still entrenched will change their ways, and accept that the rules apply to everyone. Until it is clear that this is indeed happening, it is impossible to say whether the SIB will prove any more successful in improving the standards of honesty and integrity in the City than the self-regulatory bodies which went before it. As we saw in an earlier chapter, it is equally likely that the Self-Regulatory Organisations will evolve into new forms of the old elitist hierarchy which has long been the prevalent form of regulation in the City.

Management. The reorganisation of the financial markets and the grouping of formerly small independent houses into large financial conglomerates created a hitherto unforeseen need for management in the securities industry. This had not been apparent in its cottage industry days when, under the protection of cartels, the main function of senior personnel was to develop contacts and bring in business. But the switch towards worldwide trading of equities, and the need to make markets in both equities and bonds, rather than simply acting as an agent for their purchase or sale, meant putting capital at risk every day. It required financial and technical management of a very high degree.

Management capable of handling such problems was in chronically short supply in the months after Big Bang. But there were those who envisaged a massive shakeout in the securities industry, similar to that which had occurred in America, where in the four years after its deregulation in 1975 the number of securities houses plummeted. The firms which came through this debacle were those with the strongest management, and to the extent that the pattern would repeat itself in Britain, the problem was seen to be self-correcting. It is unlikely, however, that the majority of those survivors will be native British houses. Subsidiaries of foreign institutions are sufficiently well established for the London market never again to be a playground for exclusively British firms.

Technology. British firms also face a massive challenge in their ability to adapt and develop the technology needed to support them in a world securities market. In the months before Big Bang, City firms spent unprecedented sums running collectively into hundreds of millions of pounds to equip dealing rooms and adapt to the computer-fed screen-based stock market trading system which was destined to replace the face-to-face contacts of the Stock Exchange floor. But this investment coincided with a squeeze of profits as a consequence of the abolition of fixed commissions on stock market trading, and as a result few firms seemed likely to generate adequate returns on the capital they employed in the business. They were potentially unlikely to be able to finance enhancements of their systems, and stood in grave danger of losing out to better capitalised foreign firms like Nomura of Japan, and to a lesser extent the investment houses of New York, all of which spent huge sums on research to develop systems which would respond faster, and in a more versatile way, to changes in the market place and give them a competitive edge in trading.

British firms were on a technology treadmill but did not seem to realise the full implications of this. As a consequence, they are distinctly vulnerable to the threat that their foreign competitors may turn out to be better equipped and drive them from the market place.

Politics. In the 1980s the City also came face to face with a major political challenge. For the first time it had to grapple with the prospect of parliamentary regulation which could inhibit its growth, and force it to discard long cherished ways of doing business.

For the first time it came to realise that it was held in low esteem at Westminster, not simply by its political opponents, the Labour Party, but also by many of those on the Conservative side whom it had long assumed to be its friends. Relations with the various Thatcher administrations were strained, the City resenting new windfall taxes imposed by government, government being appalled at the electoral liability the City could become if it allowed its venal side full rein in the massive salaries it paid its practitioners, and at the same time appeared outwardly to encourage dishonesty by its failure to police its markets effectively.

The challenge for the City in the late 1980s is therefore to build all-party support, so that any government, whether Conservative or Labour, will see the City as a national asset to be nurtured and promoted. But the legacy of decades of indifference to politics and politicians, cou-

pled with the diminished status of its main lobbyist, the
Bank of England, means that this is not something which
will be quickly accomplished, if indeed it can be accomplished at all. The threat of a political backlash leading to
severe curbs on the City and its businesses remains in the
1980s as one of the major threats to its development.

The social challenge.   Hand in hand with the disillusion
felt by politicians went the disillusion felt by businessmen.
The decade of the 1980s saw an unprecedented wave of
takeover activity, followed by a sharp increase in the speed
with which shares turned over on the Stock Exchange, and
a shortening of the time that investing institutions were
prepared to hold on to shares in a company. As a result,
businessmen have begun to think of the City as little
better than a casino, in which the chips that are thrown on
the roulette wheel are solid industrial assets. They have
been powerless themselves to provoke a backlash, but have
found powerful support in Parliament for those who want
the excesses of the City curbed.

   To counter this threat the City needs to develop its role
as a supporter of industry and as a champion of good
management, using its power as a shareholder to ensure
that company boards run their businesses to their max-
imum potential, and seeing that boards are strengthened if
this does not happen. But the structures and organisation
of the City were such that those institutional fund managers with the power to handle such a role rarely had the
time or the inclination to take on the burden. As a result,
the opportunity that the City had to show that it could be a
positive and constructive force for regeneration of British
industry have gone by default.

Competition.   Another handicap which the City needs to
overcome is how to be a world force when the economy in
which it is rooted is distinctly second-rate. The history of
financial power shows that it devolves to those centres
which have industrial power. That is where the capital
accumulates, and surplus capital is the fuel of the financial
markets. This explains the rise of London in the first place,

and later the rise of New York, and the emergence of Tokyo in the late 1980s as the financial centre which by the year 2000 was likely to dwarf all others. Against the overwhelming muscle of Japan and the United States, the British houses were relying on their traditional skills as deal-makers and as traders.

The more far-sighted executives in the City realise that brains alone will not be enough to ward off the City's powerful rivals. In addition, the City needs to harness the industrial muscle of continental Europe, and establish itself as the natural financial centre for the region. Though there is no obvious rival which can offer the range of services available in the City, there is a considerable groundswell of nationalist opposition and local rivalry to be overcome in centres like Paris, Frankfurt, Zurich and Milan. In addition, the history of European integration and co-operation against external economic forces has not been good. The City therefore faces a long grinding struggle to maintain its position.

Marketing. The final challenge the City faces is how to market its services. Its years of prosperity locked in cosy cartels have made it flabby, and it has no experience of having to sell financial products to a sceptical public. But the growth of competition in its traditional areas of activity, and the demands of the public for sophisticated financial advice, combine to create a major marketing opportunity. Again, however, in the 1980s the potential has rarely been perceived and the opportunity rarely grasped. As the 1980s draw to a close the major force in personal finance in Britain is the building society, not the City investment house.

Conclusion

A leading American stockbroker, Bill Schreyer of Merrill Lynch, has argued that to survive in the 1990s an investment house will need three things – the people, the capital and the will.[22] This book has been about people, and there is no doubt that the City possesses some of the most acute financial minds in the world, as well as its share of the more obtuse. It is easy to believe therefore that London has the people to ensure that it will continue as an international financial centre.

The arrival of the banks, both British and foreign, in the British securities industry also means that there is a surfeit of capital available for the markets. Some of this will be lost, but one person's loss will most probably be another's gain, so that the most natural development in the late 1980s is towards fewer and very much larger houses, each with sufficient capital for its needs.

It is the third ingredient of success which carries the biggest question mark. The City has never had to fight for its prosperity as it will have to fight in the years between now and the end of the twentieth century, and since there is no record of coping with such ferocious competition there is no means of judging how successful it will be. Nor can the City do it alone. If it is to survive and prosper it will need the support and understanding of the rest of the country, a support which, largely through the City's arrogance, has not been there in the past. But times have changed and the City has changed too. It would be a national loss of major proportions if the City were now to fail to hold its own on the world stage through a failure of national will.

Notes

Chapter 1 Can the City Survive?

1. Anonymous banker, quoted by Christopher Fildes in *The Daily Telegraph*, 25 January 1987.
2. Author's interview of 22 June 1985 with senior partner of large stockbroking house which had held talks with the Japanese.
3. Christopher Johnson, 'A Tale of Three Cities', *Lloyds Bank International Economic Review*, March 1987.

Chapter 2 The Old Fighting the New

1. Author's interview with Sir Peter Tapsell, 22 May 1985.
2. Author's interview with Michael Belmont, partner of Cazenove, 25 March 1986.
3. Author's interview with anonymous Cazenove broker, 25 March 1986.
4. Interview with Belmont, loc. cit.
5. Author's interview with anonymous managing director of middle-sized market-making firm, 29 September 1986.
6. Ibid.
7. Lindsay Vincent, 'Rowe & Pitman', *The Observer*, 27 March 1983. The Fleming was Ian, who later gave up writing brokers' circulars to create James Bond.
8. Author's interview with anonymous research director of middle-ranking stockbroker, 29 September 1986.
9. Author's interview with Mervyn Greenway, director, Capel Cure Myers, stockbrokers, 10 November 1986.
10. Author's interview with Adam Fleming, 5 December 1985.
11. Author's interview with Geoffrey Musson, 25 February 1987.
12. Author's interview with Tom Wilmot, 11 February 1987.
13. Jacques Attali, *A Man of Influence: Sir Siegmund Warburg*, Weidenfeld and Nicolson, 1986, pp. 210–15.

14. Cary Reich, 'The confessions of Siegmund Warburg', *Institutional Investor*, March 1980.

Chapter 3 Who Makes the Rules?

1. Author's interview with Roger Gibbs of Gerrard and National, 24 February 1986.
2. Author's interview with Anthony Solomons, chief executive of Singer and Friedlander, 28 October 1985.
3. Author's interview with Hitoshi Tonomura, London head of Nomura Securities, 15 January 1986.
4. Greenmail is the name given to what is in effect blackmail, except that the victim has done nothing wrong. A predator buys a large share stake in a company, then threatens to take it over. The target company then buys his shares off him at an inflated price, not available to other shareholders, in order to secure its independence. The greenmailer gains at the expense of the other shareholders, who are left with an investment in a weakened company.
5. Author's interview of 31 October 1985 with Martin Harris, Director General of Takeover Panel, 1974–6.
6. Author's interview with Gary Klesh of Quadrex, 5 June 1986.
7. Author's interview with Robert Conway of Goldman Sachs, 17 December 1985.
8. Author's interview with Ivan Boesky, 25 March 1986.
9. Author's interview with John Elliot, 23 October 1985.
10. Author's interview with Imperial board adviser, 1 December 1985.
11. Author's interview with Stanley Berwin, senior partner of S.J. Berwin, solicitors, 22 September 1986.
12. David Walker, Executive Director of the Bank of England, speech to Glasgow Finance and Investment Seminar, 24 October 1985.
13. Author's interview with Alec Monk, chief executive of Dee Corporation, 28 October 1986.
14. David Walker, loc. cit.
15. James Gower, *Review of Investor Protection*, HMSO, January 1984.
16. Sir Kenneth Berrill, interviewed in 'The Business Programme', on Channel 4 television, 1 February 1987.
17. Jonathan Confino, 'Imro confident of attracting major banks', *Daily Telegraph*, 15 March 1987.
18. Ibid.
19. *Report of the Appeal Commissioner — LHW Futures*, published by the Bank of England and the Association of Futures Brokers and Dealers, 16 March 1987.

Chapter 4 Missed Opportunities

1. Author's interview with Michael Von Clemm, head of Merrill Lynch Capital Markets, 15 January 1987.

2. The market was originally called the Eurodollar market because it was formed by US dollar balances which accumulated in London as a result of the American aid programmes to Europe after the Second World War. These were retained in London rather than repatriated because interest rates were higher there, and gradually they came to be re-lent. The term was then extended to embrace any currency or bond traded in a market other than that of its country of origin.

3. Quoted in Adrian Hamilton, *The Financial Revolution*, Viking, 1986, p. 130.

4. *Mercury Asset Management Stock Exchange Prospectus* for public issue of shares, March 1987, p. 10.

5. Author's interview with Sir Peter Tapsell of James Capel, 22 May 1985.

6. Monopolies and Mergers Commission, *Report on Proposed Merger between Smith Brothers Ltd/Bisgood, Bishop & Co.*, 1977.

7. Author's interview with Hunt Taylor, President, New York Cotton Exchange, 8 January 1986.

8. Reported in *The Independent*, 10 March 1987. The LCE was later renamed the London Futures and Options Exchange.

9. Author's interview with Brian Williamson, Chairman of Liffe, 15 April 1985.

Chapter 5 How Honest is the City?

1. Reported by Peter Rodgers in *The Guardian*, 28 February 1987.

2. Author's interview with Christopher Castleman, then chief executive of Hill Samuel, 28 October 1986.

3. *The Financial Times*, 12 March 1987, p. 1.

4. *The Financial Times*, 4 March 1987, p. 1.

5. *The Financial Times*, 27 March 1987, p. 1.

6. *The Financial Times*, 12 March 1987, p. 1.

7. Sir Nicholas Goodison, Presidential lecture to the Insurance Institute of London, 4 February 1985.

8. *Mercury Asset Management Prospectus*, Review of operations issued in March 1987.

9. Author's interview with Tony Cole, chief executive, Atlanta Fund Managers, 7 May 1986.

10. Report by Iain Scarlett and Tony Dawe, *Daily Express*, 12 October 1985.

11. *Sunday Times Business News*, 9 September 1985.

12. Author's interview with anonymous chairman of a merchant bank, 12 September 1985.

13. See Andrew Alexander, *Daily Mail*, 28 November 1985 for a full account of this matter.

14. John Roberts, 'Big Bang for the Broker Trusts', *Unit Trust Management*, April 1986, pp. 13–19.

15. *Draft Rules of Securities and Investments Board*, published 26 February 1986.

16. Sir Kenneth Newman as reported in the London *Evening Standard*, 24 March 1987.
17. Bank of England Press release, 25 March 1987.
18. Author's SEC briefing, 29 January 1987.
19. Author's interview with the Director of the corporate finance department at a leading merchant bank, 23 March 1987.

Chapter 6 City and Government
1. Susan Strange, *Sterling and British Policy*, Oxford University Press, 1971, p. 50.
2. Margaret Reid, *The Secondary Banking Crisis 1973–75*, Macmillan, 1982.
3. 'Competition and Credit Control', *Bank of England Quarterly Review*, June 1971.
4. Reid, op. cit., p. 31.
5. Douglas Jay, *Sterling. A Plea for Moderation*, Sidgwick and Jackson, 1985, pp. 148–52.
6. Ibid.
7. *Report of the Committee to Review the Functioning of the Financial Institutions*, Cmnd 7937, HMSO, 1980, p. 335.
8. Author's interview with Lord Donoughue, head of investment research at the securities house, Kleinwort Grieveson, and formerly personal adviser to Prime Minister Harold Wilson, 23 October 1984.
9. Author's interview with Sir Alfred Sherman, a political adviser to Prime Minister Thatcher, 11 June 1985.
10. Author's interview with Sir Peter Tapsell, 22 May 1985.

Chapter 7 The City and Foreign Policy
1. Paul Ferris, *Gentlemen of Fortune*, Weidenfeld and Nicolson, 1985, pp. 191–3.
2. Ibid., p. 180.
3. Roy Assersohn, *The Biggest Deal — Bankers, Politics and the Hostages of Iran*, Methuen, 1982.

Chapter 8 The City and Industry
1. Sir Nicholas Goodison, speech to the University of Aston, 28 January 1986.
2. Sir Nicholas Goodison, quoted in *The Independent*, 12 February 1987.
3. Ibid.
4. Author's interview with Christopher Roshier, Director, corporate finance, Hill Samuel, 23 March 1987.
5. Macmillan Committee, *Report on Finance and Industry*, Cmd 3897, HMSO, 1931.
6. Radcliffe Committee, *Report on the Working of the Monetary System*, Cmnd 827, HMSO, 1959.

7. Wilson Committee, *Report of the Committee to Review the Functioning of the Financial Institutions*, Cmnd 7937, HMSO 1980.

8. Ibid., p. 271.

9. Robin Leigh-Pemberton, speech at Candover Dinner, 9 October 1984.

10. Chancellor of the Exchequer Nigel Lawson, speech 'British Capitalism Resurgent' delivered at Stock Exchange, 26 September 1985.

11. Rt Hon. Nicholas Edwards speech at Cardiff Seminar on 'How to raise venture capital', 8 March 1985.

12. Robin Leigh-Pemberton, speech to British Institute of Management, 15 May 1985.

13. Lloyds Bank, *International Financial Outlook*, No. 57, 10 December 1986.

14. Author's interview with Stanislas Yassukovich, 29 September 1985.

15. Lord King, House of Lords Debate on the Finance Bill, Hansard, *House of Lords Debates*, 25 July 1984.

16. Public Accounts Committee, 10th Report, HMSO, 1982.

17. Author's interview with Gerry Grimstone of Schroders, formerly Treasury official in charge of privatisation programme, 2 March 1987.

18. Warren Taylor, managing director of Aircall, 'Going Public: the reality after the event', speech at Business International Conference, 30 April 1985.

19. Trevor Swete, quoted in 'Who pays for flotation premiums', *Financial Decisions*, December 1986.

20. Ken West, Finance Director Thames Television, 'The Pricing of New Issues', paper presented at Institute for International Research Conference, 26 March 1987.

21. Author's interview with David Prosser, head CIN — the Coal Board Pension Fund managers, 1 November 1985.

22. Shareholders' offer document pursuant to bid for Imperial Group, published by Hanson Trust in March 1986.

23. Author's interview with Peter Laister, former chief executive, Thorn EMI, 18 April 1985.

24. Author's interview with Sir Graham Wilkins, chief executive, Thorn EMI, 2 December 1985.

25. Leigh-Pemberton, speech to British Institute of Management, loc. cit.

26. Author's interview with Sir Ronnie McIntosh of APV, 8 May 1986.

27. Dr John Constable, Director General of the British Institute of Management, speech to the Society for Long Range Planning, 29 January 1986.

28. Author's interview with George Magan, Director of corporate finance, Morgan Grenfell, 15 May 1986.

29. *Acquisitions Monthly*, Review of the year, March 1986.

30. *Business Week*, 16 September 1985.

31. Leigh-Pemberton, speech to British Institute of Management, loc. cit.

32. David Walker, Executive Director of the Bank of England, speech to Glasgow Finance and Investment Seminar, 24 October 1985.

33. Leigh-Pemberton, speech at Candover Dinner, loc. cit.

34. Lawson, 'British Capitalism Resurgent', loc. cit.

35. John Coyne in *Acquisitions Monthly*, November 1985.

36. Author's interview with David Hopkinson, former chief executive M and G, 8 February 1987.

37. Walker, speech to Glasgow seminar, loc. cit.

38. Author's interview with Sir Francis Tombs, chairman of Rolls Royce and chairman Turner and Newall, 28 August 1986.

39. Author's interview with Trevor Swete, Director of corporate finance, Hill Samuel, 23 March 1987.

40. Ibid.

41. Author's interview with David Hopkinson, loc. cit.

42. P. W. Simon, investment manager Legal and General Assurance, paper presented at Institute for International Research Conference on Institutional Roles, Attitudes and Expectations, 19 September 1985.

43. Leigh-Pemberton, speech at Candover dinner, loc. cit.

Chapter 9 Is the City Good for Britain?

1. Maurice E. Button, *Helping the City to Succeed*, Bow Publications, 1986.

2. Ibid.

3. David Shepherd, 'Assessing the Consequences of Overseas Investment', *The Royal Bank of Scotland Review*, January 1987.

4. TUC, *Report on the City*, published 20 October 1986.

5. Bank of England press notice, *Institutional Investment: first Quarter 1986*.

6. Hansard, *House of Commons Debates*, 17 March 1987.

7. Reported in *The Times*, 15 March 1985.

8. TUC, op. cit., p. 33.

9. The Barings even provide a link between the Princess of Wales and the former editor of *Private Eye*, Richard Ingrams; both have a great-grandmother who was a Baring.

10. Godfrey Hodgson, *Lloyd's of London, A Reputation at Risk*, Allen Lane, 1984, pp. 108–12.

11. Author's interview with Dr Paul Neild, Head of Equities at Phillips and Drew, 20 October 1986.

12. Sunday Times/MORI City survey reported in *The Sunday Times*, 15 February 1987.

13. Author's interview with David Hardy, chairman of Globe Investment Trust, 24 March 1987.

14. BEAMA press release issued on behalf of Gorden Gaddes, 9 October 1986.

15. Anonymous merchant banker cited in Pual Ferris, *Gentlemen of Fortune*, Weidenfeld and Nicolson, 1985, p. 180.

16. David Wainwright, *Henderson, A history of the life of Alexander Henderson, First Lord Faringdon, and of Henderson Administration*, Quiller Press, 1985, p. 35.

17. *Investors Chronicle*, June 1986.

18. TUC, op. cit., p. 16.

19. David Tucker, 'The Role of the Investor', *Catalyst*, Vol. 2, No. 1, Spring 1986, p. 77.

20. Dr John Constable, Director General of the British Institute of Management, speech to Society for Long Range Planning, 29 January 1986.

21. Author's interview with anonymous director of corporate finance department of a leading Acceptance House, 23 March 1987.

22. Author's interview with William Schreyer, chairman, Merrill Lynch, 25 November 1985.

INDEX

LHW Futures, 50
Life Offices Association, 33
Lippett, John, 122
Lloyd, Richard, 44
Lloyd's of London, 1, 2, 6, 57–8, 62,
   63, 121, 122, 161, 162, 169, 179
Lloyds Bank 3, 76, 128, 133
loans, 6, 12, 30, 37, 107, 129, 133, 142
local authorities, 12, 80
London Commodity Exchange, 2, 73
London Metal Exchange, 73
Lord, Alan, 122
lunch, 20–1
Lyons, Sir Bernard, 156

M and G, 155, 176
MacDonald, Ramsay, 105
Macmillan Committee, 139
Magan, George, 23
management, company, 42–3, 150,
   151, 155–9, 180; buyouts, 154
marketing, 73, 183
Marsh and McLennan, 57
Maudling, Reginald, 119
Maxwell, Robert, 39
McGregor, John, 119
McMahon, Sir Kit, 132
Mecca, 154
Megarry, Mr Justice, 167
Mercury Asset Management, 63, 94,
   172
Merrill Lynch, 36, 55, 69, 86, 143
Midland Bank, 11, 43, 76, 122, 142
MIM group, 30
Mocatta and Goldsmid, 74
monetary policy/monetarism, 31,
   109–12
Monk, Alec, 41–2, 149
Monopolies Commission, 68, 153
Montagu, Samuel, 43, 74, 76, 122,
   128
Morgan, John, 49
Morgan, J.S., 131
Morgan Grenfell, 23, 24, 36, 28, 40,
   61, 76, 86, 120, 122, 128, 131, 177
Morgan Guaranty, 55
Mortimer, Kate, 121
Mountain family, 16
Mullens, 35, 36
Murphy, Sir Leslie, 116
Musson, Geoffrey, 24–5

National Insurance and Guarantee
   Corporation, 97
National Union of Mineworkers, 167
National Westminster Bank, 11, 23,
   76, 119
Nationalisation Act (1946), 112

Neild, Dr Paul, 170
Nelson, John, 158
new issues, 12, 96–9, 142–7, 157
New London Oil, 98–9
New York, 6, 13, 48, 53, 62, 66, 152,
   183
Newman, Sir Kenneth, 102
Nissen, George, 36
Nomura Securities, 55, 181
Norman, Sir Montagu, 104–5, 123
Northern Ireland, 138
Norton Warburg, 46
Norwich Union, 120
Nott, Sir John, 119

O'Brien, Lord, 107
Office of Fair Trading, 108
oil, 99, 109, 127. 132; North Sea, 164,
   166, 167
OPEC, 134
options, 152; currency-traded, 75
Orion Royal Bank, 120
overdrafts, bank, 147
overseas earnings, 62–3, 160–2, 165,
   167
overseas investment, 59, 62–3, 141,
   161, 163–8; portfolio, 163–5
ownership, share, 143, 144, 169;
   Stock Exchange, 67, 68

Palliser, Sir Michael, 122
Panama, 128
Parkinson, Cecil, 108
Parnes, Tony, 90
pension funds, 41, 63, 95–6, 147, 153,
   155, 164–5, 175
Pepper, Gordon, 110
Pertamina, 128
Phillips and Drew, 61, 75, 170, 171
Pilkington, 154
placings, 96–7
Poland, 134–5
politics/politicians, 3, 7, 20–1, 114–
   21, 123, 126, 144, 174, 181–2 *see
   also individual headings*
prices, 5, 24–6, 80, 84–92, 97, 102,
   103, 142–6, 149, 156–8, 177;
   premium, 145, 146
Prideaux, Sir John, 23
Prior, James, 120
privatisation, 98, 102, 121, 127, 144,
   169
privilege, 160, 168–71 *see also*
   elitism
property, 96, 107
Pru Bache, 40
Prudential, 45, 155, 156
Prussia, 129–31 *passim*

individual headings
Stonehouse, John, 120
Stuttaford, William, 45
Swan Hunter, 173
swaps market, 31
Swete, Trevor, 146
Swid, 40
Swire, 117, 118
Swiss Banking Corporation, 61
Switzerland, 55, 56, 61; Union Bank
of, 55, 56, 61, 171
Sykes, Richard, 45

takeovers, 4, 5, 19, 24–7, 30, 36–41,
81, 83–7, 103, 148–54, 157, 159,
176–7, 182; Panel, 5, 19, 36–40,
150–1
Tapsell, Sir Peter, 16–17, 118
Tate and Lyle, 117, 118
taxation, 5, 65, 169, 181
technical experts, 139
technology, 69, 180–1
telecommunications, 59, 66
Thames Television, 146
Thatcher, Margaret, 3, 31, 109, 110,
112, 124, 132, 133
Thorn EMI, 149, 158
time horizons, investment, 4, 151–3,
176, 182
Tokyo, 6, 12, 12, 34, 35, 53, 59, 182
Tombs, Sir Francis, 42, 155, 158
trade, 134, 142
Trade and Industry, Department of,
5, 25, 46, 86, 177; Secretary of
State for, 47
Trafalgar House, 149
Transamerica Corporation, 58
Treasury, 31, 104, 106, 107, 111–12,
121, 123, 125, 144, 166, 167
Trinder, A.W., 16
TUC, 164, 166, 174
Tucker, David, 176
Tuke family, 16
Turkey, 128
Turner and Newall, 42, 155, 158

UDS, 156
underwriting, 41, 54, 94, 97, 143
Union Discount, 76, 77

unit trusts, 63, 94–5, 100, 152;
Association, 37
United States, 1, 3, 5, 6, 11, 12, 29,
37, 57, 72, 129, 134–5, 138, 141,
142, 146, 151, 153, 178, 183;
Federal Reserve Board, 105, 112,
133; hostage crisis, 3, 4, 132;
Securities and Exchange
Commission, 31, 47, 48, 51, 86,
102; Treasury, 106

Vaskevich, Nahum, 86
Venezuela, 128
Vickers Da Costa, 66

Wales, 140
Walker, David, 108, 152, 155
Wall Street, 3, 34, 53, 64, 87, 102
Warburg, S.G., 25, 36, 38, 42, 76,
119, 122, 128
Warburg, Sir Siegmund, 25–7, 54,
171
Ward White, 39
Wedd Durlacher, 35, 36, 70
Westland, 32
Westmacott, Richard, 45
Whitehall, 3, 7, 8, 31, 46, 112, 113,
121–3, 147
Wilcox, Malcolm, 43
Wilhelm, Prince, 131
Wilkins, Sir Graham, 149
Williams, Lord, 22, 30, 116
Williamson, Brian, 118
Willis Faber, 116, 117
Wilmot, Tom, 25
Wilson, Harold (Lord), 108, 120;
Committee, 108, 139, 141
Wilson, Nicholas, 45
Wolfson, Sir Isaac, 149
Wood Mackenzie, 170, 171
Woolworth, 159
World Bank, 129
World War, First, 3, 104, 131, 166;
Second, 1, 3

Yassukovich, Stanislas, 143

Zaire, 128
Zambia, 128
Zurich, 6, 183